Library Use of eBooks,
2013 Edition

ISBN: 978-1-57440-223-0
Library of Congress Control Number: 2013932534
© 2013 Primary Research Group, Inc.

TABLE OF CONTENTS

SURVEY PARTICIPANTS

Alamogordo Public Library
Alberta AIM Library Services
Alberta Innovates - Technology Futures Libraries
Anaheim Public Library
Association of American Medical Colleges
Australian Department of Foreign Affairs and Trade
Australian Department of Innovation, Industry, Science and Research
Bay of Plenty District Health Board
Benton County Public Library
Brentwood City Library
Canterbury Christ Church University
Capital Health Hospitals
Cedar Crest College
Central Mississippi Regional Library System
Charter College
Cirencester College
Clay County Public Library
Coastal Carolina University
College of the Holy Cross
Dar Al-Hekma College
Fairbanks North Star Borough Library
Florida Keys Community College
Francisco Marroquín University
Galway Public Library
George C. Marshall European Center for Security Studies
Georgetown Public Library
Hancock County Library System
Houston Public Library
Jersey Shore University Medical Center
Johnson C. Smith University
Jülich Research Centre
Kalispell Regional Medical Center
Lansing Community College
Lewis County Public Library
Luther Seminary
Master's College
Mercer County Community College
Monterey Peninsula College
Nanyang Technological University
Newcastle Public Library
Niagara College
Old Dominion University
Parkersburg and Wood County Public Library

Parkview Health
Pellissippi State Community College
Phillips 66 Company
Renton Technical College
Sacramento Public Library
Saginaw Valley State University
Saint Mary's College
Sharon Public Library
Simpson College
Smith, Anderson, Blount, Dorsett, Mitchell and Jernigan, LLP
Smith, Gambrell and Russell, LLP
State Library of Victoria
Stockton-San Joaquin County Public Library
Treat Memorial Library
United States Sports Academy
University of Auckland
University of Connecticut
University of Massachusetts Amherst
University of Memphis
University of New Hampshire School of Law
University of Portsmouth
University of Wisconsin-La Crosse
Villanova University
Wartburg Public Library
Yanbu Industrial College

THE QUESTIONNAIRE

1. Please provide the contact information requested below.
    Personal Name:
    Organization:
    Email Address:
    Phone Number:

2. Which phrase best describes your organization?
    (a) Public Library
    (b) College Library
    (c) Corporate or Legal Library
    (d) Government, Association or State Library
    (e) Other (please specify)

3. What is the total approximate annual budget of your library for all purposes including buildings, salaries, materials and all other costs?

4. What is/will be the library's total spending on e-books, including database contracts and purchases, in each of the following academic or calendar years? Exclude spending on hardware.
    2012:
    2013:

5. Does the library have a current contract for e-books from any of the following vendors?
    (a) NetLibrary/EBSCO
    (b) Palgrave/Macmillan
    (c) Safari
    (d) McGraw-Hill eBook Library
    (e) ABC-CLIO
    (f) Amazon
    (g) eBook Library/Baker & Taylor
    (h) SciVerse ScienceDirect
    (i) Ellibs
    (j) OverDrive
    (k) Follett Higher Education Group
    (l) MyiLibrary
    (m) Ebrary
    (n) Knovel
    (o) Lecture Notes in Computer Science
    (p) EBL
    (q) Gale Virtual Reference Library
    (r) Bookish
    (s) Wiley Online Library
    (t) SwetsWise

6. How many existing e-book licensing contracts does the library have with individual publishers or aggregators?

7. What are a few of your favorite e-book suppliers and why do you like them?

8. What percentage of the e-book contracts that your library currently has do you expect to renew upon completion of the current contract?

9. How much did your library spend in the past year on e-books or e-documents from the following vendors in the past year? If you have not spent anything on e-books from these vendors then enter "0".
 Amazon:
 Barnes & Noble:
 Google:
 Other Online Book Vendors:

10. What percentage of the library's total spending on e-books was with the following type of vendor? For example, Amazon or NetLibrary would be considered aggregators while John Wiley & Sons would be an individual publisher.
 Aggregators:
 Individual Publishers:

11. What percentage of the number of these separate contracts (not their value or size) does the library have with each specific type of vendor?
 Aggregators:
 Individual Publishers:

12. What percentage of the library's total e-book ordering was made through the following channels? We are asking who you order from and pay the bill to.
 (a) Through e-book divisions of a traditional book jobber or book distributor such as EBSCO's NetLibrary or Baker & Taylor's eBook Library and other such divisions
 (b) Through an electronic information aggregator not connected to a major book jobber or distributor
 (c) Direct from a publisher

13. What percentage of the library's e-book collection spending is through contracts negotiated by consortium?

14. What provisions have you made to help your patrons find and download or otherwise utilize the many e-books in the public domain that are now available?

15. What was the library's total spending on e-audio books in the following years?
 2012:
 2013:

16. How many e-audio book titles are currently offered by your library?

17. If your library currently offers e-audio book titles, by what percentage will the number of e-audio books offered by the library change over the next year?

18. Has the library ever used e-book rental or e-book interlibrary loan sites which enable patrons to have access to an e-book for a fee for a brief specified time period, often 30-60 days?
    (a) Yes
    (b) No

19. How much did the library spend exclusively on "borrowing rights" to e-books, defined as any model that compels you to pay per time borrowed rather than for unlimited rights or rights to a certain number of viewings for a set fee?

20. Do you think that you might be interested in this kind of site?
    (a) Yes
    (b) No

21. What percentage of the top 20 titles loaned out to patrons of your library in the last year are also available for loan in e-book format?

22. In what areas is your library most anxious to build its e-book collection?

23. Does the library own a stand-alone e-book reading device of any kind (PC's and workstations not included)?
    (a) Yes
    (b) No

24. Does the library currently own or lease any of the following to provide e-books to patrons or staff?
    (a) Amazon Kindle
    (b) Apple iPad
    (c) Barnes & Noble Nook
    (d) BlackBerry PlayBook
    (e) Franklin eBookMan
    (f) Motorola Xoom
    (g) Samsung Galaxy
    (h) Sony Reader
    (i) Other

25. Does the library plan to acquire any of the following within the next year?
    (a) Amazon Kindle
    (b) Apple iPad
    (c) Barnes & Noble Nook
    (d) BlackBerry PlayBook
    (e) Franklin eBookMan
    (f) Motorola Xoom

(g) Samsung Galaxy
(h) Sony Reader
(i) Other

26. How much did/will your library spend on dedicated e-book readers and tablet computers in the specified years?
2012:
2013:

27. For approximately what percentage of the e-books in the library's collection would you estimate that the library also has a corresponding print copy?

28. If the library has an endowment, bequest, or specially dedicated fund of any kind for books, may this fund be used for the purchase of e-books?
(a) Yes, we have a special endowment for books but we cannot use it for e-books
(b) Yes, we have a special endowment for books and we can use it for e-books
(c) We have an endowment especially for e-books or other electronic/internet resources
(d) No, we have no such endowment for books of any kind

29. How would you describe your use of e-books for course reserve?
(a) Not really used at all
(b) Scant use
(c) Modest use
(d) Significant use
(e) Accounts for more than half of all book use on Course Reserves

30. Has the use of e-books for electronic course reserves increased or decreased over the past two years? What are the current constraints on use and what do you expect for the near future?

31. How much did the library spend on electronic and/or internet versions of directories in the past year?

32. How much does the library plan to spend on electronic and/or internet versions of directories in the upcoming year?

33. In the past year what has been the library's experience with changes in the prices of e-books relative to the changes in price of traditional print books and online databases of full text articles?

E-Books Relative to Print Books
(a) Price increases have been about the same
(b) Price increases have been higher for e-books
(c) Our e-book prices have not increased

E-Books Relative to Online Full Text Databases
    (a) Price increases have been about the same
    (b) Price increases have been higher for e-books
    (c) Our e-book prices have not increased

34. What was the average percentage change in e-book prices that your organization paid in the last year?

35. Discuss your library's e-book collection strategy. How fast do you expect your e-book collection to grow? Has it led to reduced spending on traditional books? Do your library patrons make use of e-book searching capacity? How will e-books affect your cataloging and information literacy strategies?

36. Do internet enabled tablets such as the Apple iPad, the HP Slate, or any of the Google Tablets figure in your e-book planning? Will you use the e-book capabilities of these devices in your library in the near future?

37. Well known websites, newspapers and other media outlets such as The New York Times and the Huffington Post have started to publish and sell their own e-books. Has your library purchased e-books from these types of sites?

38. Describe your library's attempts to license e-textbooks. Have you approached or negotiated with any textbook publishers over e-book rights? What kind of results have you achieved? Do you have plans or a strategy in this area?

39. How much did your library spend on purchasing, leasing or licensing e-textbooks in the years listed below?
    2012:
    2013:

SUMMARY OF MAIN FINDINGS

Total Spending on E-Books

Libraries in the sample spent a mean of $118,676 on e-books in 2012, with libraries in the United States spending a mean of $53,759. Public libraries in the sample spent approximately $52,424 on e-books in 2012, whereas college libraries spent a mean of $122,920 and other libraries spent $185,275. In 2013, libraries in the sample will spend a mean of $130,053 on e-books, nearly 10% more than the year prior. College libraries will increase spending by $28,333, to a mean of $151,753, and public libraries will increase spending to a mean of $53,378. Libraries in the sample with a total annual budget of less than $500,000 will spend about $43,814 on e-books in 2013, 25% more than in the previous year, while libraries with a budget between $500,000 and $4 million will reduce e-book spending by a mean of $16,619 or 17%.

E-Book Contracts

40% of libraries in the sample have a current contract for e-books with NetLibrary/EBSCO, making it one of the most utilized e-book vendors in the survey. 44.44% of libraries in the United States and 30% of libraries in other countries have an e-book contract with NetLibrary/EBSCO, including 10.53% of public libraries, 66.67% of college libraries and 22.22% of other libraries. Half of all libraries with a total annual budget of $500,000 have an e-book contract with NetLibrary/EBSCO, as do 26.92% of libraries with a budget of less than $500,000 and 44.44% of libraries with a budget over $4 million.

10% of libraries in the sample, most of them with an annual budget of more than $4 million, have a current e-book contract with Safari. 15.56% of college libraries have a Safari contract, as do 5.26% of public libraries and 5.56% of other libraries. No public libraries in the sample have a contract for e-books with McGraw-Hill eBook Library, though 15.15% of college libraries and 11.11% of other libraries do. In total, 10% of libraries in the sample have an e-book contract with McGraw-Hill, 8% of libraries in the United States and 15% of those in other countries. 5.71% of libraries in the sample have an e-book contract with ABC-CLIO and 4.29% have a contract with Lecture Notes in Computer Science.

15.71% of libraries in the sample have an e-book contract with SciVerse and 18.57% have a contract with OverDrive. The former consist of 27.27% of college libraries and 11.11% of other libraries, while the latter are made up exclusively of public libraries, 68.42% of which in the sample have a contract with OverDrive. Whereas OverDrive is used mainly by libraries in the United States, MyiLibrary is used most by libraries in other countries. 25% of libraries in other countries have an e-book contract with MyiLibrary, compared with 4% of libraries in the United States. Together these account for 10% of libraries in the sample, including 18.18% of college libraries and 5.56% of other libraries.

Ebrary e-book contracts are almost exclusively held by college libraries in the sample, 63.64% of which have a contract for e-books with this vendor. 32.86% of libraries in the sample have a contract with Ebrary, including 19.23% of libraries with a total budget of less than $500,000, 34.62% of libraries with a budget of $500,000 to $4 million and 50% of libraries with a budget of more than $4 million. 8.57% of libraries in the sample, 6% of those in the United States and 15% of those in other countries, have an e-book contract with Knovel, while 10% have a contract with EBL, including 18.18% of college libraries and 5.56% of other libraries, but 0% of public libraries.

27.14% of libraries in the sample have an e-book contract with Gale Virtual Reference Library. Most of these are libraries in the United States, 34% of which have an e-book contract with Gale, and many are college libraries, 45.45% of which do. E-book contracts with Gale Virtual Reference Library are held by 11.54% of libraries with an overall budget of less than $500,000, 26.92% of libraries with a budget of $500,000 to $4 million and 50% of libraries with a total annual budget over $4 million. 33.33% of the latter have an e-book contract with Wiley Online Library, though only 12.86% of all libraries in the sample use this vendor. 21.21% of college libraries have an e-book contract with Wiley Online Library, as do 11.11% of other libraries.

While no libraries in the sample have an e-book contract with Bookish, Ellibs or Follett Higher Education Group, 1.43% do have a contract with eBook Library/Baker and Taylor. 2.86% of libraries in the sample, including 5.26% of public libraries and 3.03% of college libraries, have an e-book contract with Amazon and the same number have a contract with Palgrave Macmillan and SwetsWise. Libraries on both ends of the budget spectrum have e-book contracts with Palgrave Macmillan, whereas all libraries with Amazon contracts have an annual budget of less than $500,000 and all those with SwetsWise contracts have a budget over $4 million.

On average, libraries in the sample have about 3.92 existing e-book licensing contracts with individual publishers or aggregators. Libraries in the United States have a mean of 3.48 such contracts, while those in other countries have a mean of 5. Public libraries average just 1.06 e-book contracts, whereas college libraries have a mean of 5.97 and other libraries have a mean of 2.56. Libraries in the sample expect to renew almost 75% of their current e-book contracts upon completion, with libraries in the United States renewing a mean of 68.46% and libraries in other countries renewing a mean of 89.06%.

Spending by Vendor

E-books from Amazon have cost libraries in the sample a mean of $358 in the past year, $85 among libraries in the United States and $1,028 among libraries in other countries. College libraries have spent a mean of $41 on e-books from Amazon and public libraries have spent a mean of $16, while other libraries have spent around $1,283 on e-books from this vendor. Libraries with an annual budget of $500,000 to $4 million have spent a mean of $822 on e-books from Amazon, whereas those with a budget of less than $500,000 have spent $148 and those with a budget of more than $4 million spent $17.

Libraries in the sample have spent a mean of $476 on e-books from Barnes & Noble in the past year. While public and college libraries have spent more on e-books from Barnes &

Noble than on those from Amazon, $116 and $327 respectively, they still lag behind other libraries, which have spent a mean of $1,111 and a maximum of $20,000. Libraries in the United States have spent a mean of $49 on e-books from Barnes & Noble, whereas those in other countries have spent a mean of $1,500. Only one library in the sample has purchased e-books from Google in the past year and it spent just $50 on these purchases.

Other online book vendors account for a mean of $11,744 in e-book purchases made by libraries in the sample. Libraries in the United States have spent a mean of $7,697 on e-books from these vendors in the past year, while libraries in other countries have spent more than $21,100. College libraries have made the most use of these vendors, spending a mean of $12,805, whereas public libraries have spent $12,341 and other libraries have spent $9,339. Libraries with a total budget under $500,000 have spent a mean of $2,414 on e-books from other online vendors, while libraries with a budget of more than $4 million have spent a mean of $35,924.

E-Book Distribution

A mean of 79.06% of total e-book spending by libraries in the sample was made through aggregators and 20.94% was made with individual publishers. Public libraries spent a mean of 99.85% of their total e-book spending with aggregators, while college libraries made 74.23% of their purchases with these vendors. 26% of e-book spending in libraries with an annual budget of less than $500,000 and nearly a quarter of this spending in libraries with a budget of more than $4 million was with individual publishers, whereas just 15% of e-book spending in libraries with a budget between $500,000 and $4 million was with publishers of this kind.

Libraries in the sample have approximately 75.42% of e-book contracts with aggregators and 24.58% of these contracts with individual publishers. Libraries in other countries have a mean of 37.57% of e-book contracts with individual publishers, while libraries in the United States have only 18.71% of their contracts with them. Public libraries have 98.08% of total e-book contracts with aggregators, compared with 72.55% of e-book contracts among college libraries and 52.3% of contracts among other libraries.

37.13% of e-book orders made by libraries in the sample are placed with e-book divisions of traditional book jobbers or distributors. 45.44% of these orders are made through an electronic information aggregator not connected to a major jobber and 16.42% are made directly from a publisher. More than half of e-book orders made by libraries in the United States are done through information aggregators not connected to a major book jobber, while 40% of orders in libraries in other countries are made through an e-book division of a major jobber or distributor. Public libraries make a mean of 85.21% of e-book orders from electronic information aggregators not affiliated with a major book jobber, whereas college libraries overwhelmingly purchase e-books from traditional book jobbers and other libraries prefer to buy e-books directly from the publisher.

Nearly 30% of e-book spending by libraries in the sample is done through contracts negotiated by consortium. This includes 31.76% of e-book spending in public libraries,

35.13% of e-book spending in college libraries and 18.89% of this spending in other libraries. Libraries with an annual budget of less than $500,000 use consortium contracts for a mean of 26.67% of their total e-book spending, whereas libraries with a budget of more than $4 million make a mean of 32.5% of e-book spending via consortium.

Audio Books

Libraries in the sample spent a mean of $2,350 on e-audio books in 2012. This spending is expected to increase to a mean of $2,438 in 2013, with libraries outside the United States spending about $275 more than in the year prior. Public libraries spent a mean of $9,969 on e-audio books in 2012, though this spending will fall slightly in the coming year, while college libraries spent a mean of $200 and expect to spend more than twice that amount in 2013. Libraries with a total annual budget of less than $500,000 will experience a similar increase in spending on e-audio books in 2013, while libraries with larger budgets will keep this spending flat.

Libraries in the sample currently offer a mean of 1,091 e-audio book titles, 1,571 titles among libraries in the United States and 30 titles among libraries abroad, and expect to increase these offerings by 4.83% in the coming year. Public libraries have a mean of 4,590 e-audio book titles and will increase these by a mean of 5.25%, whereas college libraries offer a mean of 79 e-audio book titles and plan an increase of 1.9%. Libraries with an annual budget of less than $500,000 offer a mean of 206 e-audio book titles, while those with a budget of $500,000 to $4 million offer 1,451 different e-audio books and libraries with a budget over $4 million offer a mean of 1,751.

Interlibrary Loan

E-book rental or interlibrary loan websites which enable patrons to access e-books for a fee for a specified period of time have been used by 3.17% of libraries in the sample. 46.67% of survey participants say that they may be interested in using a website of this kind, including 28.57% of participants in public libraries, 62.07% of participants in college libraries and 35.29% of participants in other libraries. In total, libraries in the sample have spent a mean of $1,062 and a maximum of $50,000 on borrowing rights for e-books. Whereas libraries in the United States have spent a mean of just $15 on borrowing rights, those in other countries have spent roughly $2,971 to this effect. College libraries are responsible for the bulk of this expenditure, with public libraries spending a mean of less than $14 on interlibrary loan borrowing rights and other libraries spending nothing at all.

Availability of Titles

Among libraries in the sample, a mean of 12.85% of the top 20 titles loaned out to patrons in the last year are available for loan in e-format. Libraries in the United States offer a mean of 15.12% of their top 20 titles as e-books, while libraries in other countries offer a mean of 7.36% of these titles electronically. Nearly 30% of the top titles in public colleges are available for loan in e-formats, as opposed to 6.96% of these titles in college libraries and 10.8% of them in other libraries. Libraries with a total budget of more than $4 million offer a mean of 25.67% of their top 20 titles in the past year in e-book form, whereas those with a budget between $500,000 and $4 million offer a mean of 7.35% of these titles in this format.

Reading Devices

50% of libraries in the sample, 52.38% of libraries in the United States and 44.44% of those in other countries, own a stand-alone e-book reading device of some kind. These include 71.43% of public libraries, 51.72% of college libraries and 29.41% of other libraries. 40% of libraries with an annual budget of less than $500,000 own one or more e-book reading devices, whereas 56% of libraries with a budget between $500,000 and $4 million and 53.33% of libraries with a budget over $4 million own a device of this kind.

Kindle e-book readers are owned or leased by 19.12% of libraries in the sample, including 22.45% of libraries in the United States and 10.53% of those in other countries. 31.58% of public libraries own or lease a Kindle, as do 12.5% of college libraries and 17.65% of other libraries. 8.82% of libraries in the sample plan to acquire a Kindle within the next year, including 12% of libraries with a total budget of less than $500,000 and 7.69% of libraries with a budget between $500,000 and $4 million. 24% of the former and 19.23% of the latter already offer Kindles to their patrons and/or staff, though less than 12% of libraries with a budget of more than $4 million do the same.

25% of college libraries and 5.26% of public libraries own or lease an Apple iPad, whereas 29.41% of other libraries have a device of this kind. Altogether, 20.59% of libraries in the sample own or a lease an iPad, many of these libraries with an annual budget over $4 million; 29.41% of libraries with a budget over $4 million own or lease an iPad, along with 26.92% of libraries with a budget of $500,000 to $4 million and 8% of libraries with a budget under $500,000. 14.71% of libraries in the sample plan to acquire an iPad over the coming year, almost all of these college libraries, 28.13% of which will do so.

13.24% of libraries in the sample own or lease a Barnes & Noble Nook, including 26.32% of public libraries and 12.5% of college libraries. Nooks are popular with libraries with an annual budget of more than $4 million or less than $500,000, but are less so among libraries with a budget between $500,000 and $4 million, of which less than 8% own or lease the device. 1.47% of libraries in the sample plan to acquire a Nook within the next year, all college libraries with a budget of less than $500,000.

Sony Readers are only marginally less popular with libraries in the sample than Nooks are, with 11.76% of libraries owning or leasing at least one. 8.16% of libraries in the United States have a Sony Reader, compared with 21.05% of libraries in other countries. These include 15.79% of public libraries, 12.5% of college libraries and 5.88% of other libraries. The Samsung Galaxy, meanwhile, is owned or leased by just 1.47% of libraries in the sample, all college libraries with a budget of more than $4 million. No libraries in the sample currently have a Blackberry Playbook, Motorola Xoom or Franklin eBookMan, nor do any have plans to acquire one of these devices within the next year.

Libraries in the sample spent a mean of $1,003 on dedicated e-book readers and tablet computers in 2012 and will spend a mean of $993 in 2013. Libraries in the United States, which spent a mean of $978 on e-book readers in 2012, will spend about $687 on these devices in the coming year. At the same time, libraries in other countries will increase spending on e-book readers and tablets from a mean of $1,056 in 2012 to approximately $1,639 in 2013. Public libraries will decrease spending on e-book readers in 2013 to a mean of $546, down roughly $954 or 63% from the year prior, while college libraries will up this spending by 48%.

Print vs. Online

Libraries in the sample have corresponding print copies for a mean of 28.11% of e-books in their collection. Libraries in the United States have print copies for a mean of 31.14% and a maximum of 100% of e-books, while libraries in other countries have them for a mean of 21.53% of e-books. Public libraries maintain print versions of 50% of e-books in their collection, whereas college libraries have print versions for a mean of 19.41%. Libraries with an annual budget of more than $4 million have print copies for 43.29% of e-books, while libraries with a budget of less than $500,000 retain print copies for 18.42% of all e-books.

While just 1.61% of libraries in the sample have an endowment, bequest or dedicated fund especially for e-books and other electronic resources, 19.35% have an endowment for books that can be used on these materials. 14.52% of libraries have an endowment that precludes the purchase of e-books, whereas 64.52% have no endowment for books of any kind. 6.67% of public libraries, all in the United States and all with a budget of $500,000 to $4 million, have an endowment especially for e-books, and 20% have an endowment that can be used for this purpose. 26.67% of college libraries also have an endowment that can be used for e-books, as do 31.25% of libraries with a total budget of more than $4 million.

Electronic Course Reserve

7.32% of survey participants report significant use of e-books for course reserve in their library, while 21.95% report modest use and 9.76% report scant use. 60.98% of survey participants say that they do not use e-books for course reserve, including 83.33% of participants in public libraries and 60% of those in college libraries. Significant use is limited to 10% of college libraries, all with total budgets of more than $4 million, while modest use is concentrated in libraries with budgets of less than $500,000. In general, survey participants have noted an increase in the use of e-books for course reserve over the past two years, with the biggest constraint on this usage being the lack of availability of certain titles or texts.

Directories

Electronic and internet directories have cost libraries in the sample a mean of $2,820 in the past year. Libraries in the United States have spent a mean of $3,267, while those in other countries have spent a mean of $1,867. Public libraries have spent a mean of $8,750 on electronic and internet versions of directories, considerably more than the $1,820 spent by college libraries or the $1,324 spent by other libraries in the sample. Libraries with an annual budget of less than $500,000 have spent a mean of $134 on electronic directories, while those with a budget of $500,000 or more have spent in excess of $4,600. Spending on electronic directories will remain relatively flat in the upcoming year, with college libraries spending somewhat less than they did in the previous year and other libraries spending somewhat more.

Pricing

In 44.44% of libraries in the sample, including 54.84% of libraries in the United States and 21.43% of those in other countries, price increases have been greater for e-books than for traditional print books. 33.33% of survey participants say that price increases for e-books and print books have been about the same over the past year, while 22.22% say that e-books have not increased in price. The latter include 25% of survey participants in libraries with a total budget under $500,000 and 31.25% of participants in libraries with a budget of $500,000 to $4 million, but just 7.69% of those in libraries with a budget of more than $4 million, the majority of which say that price increases have been higher for e-books than print books.

26.67% of survey participants say that price increases in the past year have been higher for e-books then for online full text databases, while 44.44% say that increases have been about the same. 32.26% of libraries in the United States have experienced greater price increases for e-books than for full text databases, compared with 14.29% of libraries in other countries. Whereas just 22.22% of survey participants in public libraries feel that price increases for e-books have been about the same as increases for full text databases, 47.83% of participants in college libraries and 53.85% of those in other libraries in the sample feel this way.

On average, libraries in the sample have experienced a mean increase of 17.93% in the price of e-books in the last year, though some libraries report increases of up to 200%. Libraries in the United States have experienced a 25.23% increase in the price of e-books, while libraries in other countries have seen prices increase by 4.8%. Whereas libraries with a total annual budget of less than $500,000 have experienced a somewhat moderate increase in the price of e-books, prices among libraries with an annual budget over $4 million have soared by a mean of 34.29%. Increases have been even more dramatic in public libraries, which have seen e-book prices rise by a mean of 54.17% in the last year. In contrast, e-book prices for college libraries have increased by a mean of 10.39% and prices among other libraries have increased by about 4.67%.

Collection Planning

While libraries that can afford to will maintain spending on traditional books and databases, others will cut spending in these areas to compensate for increases in e-books. Libraries in the sample are looking to build their e-books collections in a diverse number of subject areas, including many specialized fields, from welding to funeral services. In particular, libraries will expand their e-book holdings in bestsellers and popular fiction, healthcare, the social sciences and education. In addition, 1.72% of libraries have purchased e-books from well-known websites, newspapers and other media outlets such as The New York Times and the Huffington Post.

Textbooks

Most libraries in the sample do not offer e-textbooks, with many survey participants citing budget constraints and pricing issues as the sole reason. One survey participants wrote, "Publishers will not license e-textbooks to libraries. The several times that I have licensed them, I've been hit with DRACONIC DRM issues and huge price increases [...] Until publishers become library friendly, we will not be pursuing plans for e-textbooks." Other survey participants have expressed frustration with their e-book aggregators for not including enough textbooks in their offerings.

Nonetheless, spending on e-textbooks will increase from a mean of $1,042 in 2012 to approximately $1,528 in 2013. Public libraries will increase spending from $0 to $1,111 and college libraries will increase spending from $250 to $875. At the same time, other libraries will reduce spending on e-textbooks by about 5%. Libraries with an annual budget of less than $500,000 will spend a mean of $1,455 on e-textbooks in 2013 and those with a budget of $500,000 to $4 million will spend a mean of $2,381, whereas libraries with a budget over $4 million will continue to spend nothing on these materials.

CHARACTERISTICS OF THE SAMPLE

Country

	United States	Other
Entire Sample	72.06%	27.94%

Type of Library

	Public Library	College Library	Other
Entire Sample	27.94%	47.06%	25.00%

Total Library Budget

	Less than $500,000	$500,000 to $4 Million	More than $4 Million
Entire Sample	36.76%	38.24%	25.00%

CHAPTER 1: BASIC DIMENSIONS OF E-BOOK USE

Table 1: What was or will be the library's total spending on e-books in each of the following academic or calendar years?

Table 1.1: What was the library's total spending on e-books in 2012? (in $US)

Country	Mean	Median	Minimum	Maximum
Entire Sample	$118,676.34	$14,500.00	$0.00	$2,296,020.00

Table 1.2: What was the library's total spending on e-books in 2013? (in $US)

Country	Mean	Median	Minimum	Maximum
Entire Sample	$130,053.10	$15,000.00	$0.00	$3,116,009.00

Table 2: What was or will be the library's total spending on e-books in each of the following academic or calendar years? Broken out by Country

Table 2.1: What was the library's total spending on e-books in 2012? Broken out by Country (in $US)

Country	Mean	Median	Minimum	Maximum
United States	$53,759.09	$10,000.00	$0.00	$572,000.00
Other	$277,362.94	$39,303.50	$500.00	$2,296,020.00

Table 2.2: What was the library's total spending on e-books in 2013? Broken out by Country (in $US)

Country	Mean	Median	Minimum	Maximum
United States	$59,434.09	$14,500.00	$0.00	$716,000.00
Other	$302,677.33	$41,164.00	$1,000.00	$3,116,009.00

Table 3: What was or will be the library's total spending on e-books in each of the following academic or calendar years? Broken out by Type of Library

Table 3.1: What was the library's total spending on e-books in 2012? Broken out by Type of Library (in $US)

Type of Library	Mean	Median	Minimum	Maximum
Public Library	$52,423.94	$6,000.00	$0.00	$550,000.00
College Library	$122,920.13	$28,500.00	$0.00	$2,296,020.00
Other	$185,274.80	$8,200.00	$0.00	$900,000.00

Table 3.2: What was the library's total spending on e-books in 2013? Broken out by Type of Library 2013 (in $US)

Type of Library	Mean	Median	Minimum	Maximum
Public Library	$53,378.12	$12,000.00	$0.00	$550,000.00
College Library	$151,753.40	$36,500.00	$0.00	$3,116,009.00
Other	$173,550.80	$15,000.00	$0.00	$716,000.00

Table 4: What was or will be the library's total spending on e-books in each of the following academic or calendar years? Broken out by Total Library Budget

Table 4.1: What was the library's total spending on e-books in 2012? Broken out by Total Library Budget (in $US)

Library Budget	Mean	Median	Minimum	Maximum
Less than $500,000	$35,110.16	$1,500.00	$0.00	$572,000.00
$500,000 to $4 Million	$95,833.33	$14,000.00	$0.00	$900,000.00
More than $4 Million	$279,229.94	$99,786.00	$20,000.00	$2,296,020.00

Table 4.2: What was the library's total spending on e-books in 2013? Broken out by Total Library Budget (in $US)

Library Budget	Mean	Median	Minimum	Maximum
Less than $500,000	$43,813.96	$3,000.00	$0.00	$716,000.00
$500,000 to $4 Million	$79,214.29	$14,000.00	$0.00	$700,000.00
More than $4 Million	$331,527.69	$94,500.00	$13,174.00	$3,116,009.00

Table 5: Does the library have a current contract for e-books from any of the following vendors?

Table 5.1: Does the library have an e-book contract with NetLibrary/EBSCO?

	Yes	No
Entire Sample	40.00%	60.00%

Table 5.2: Does your library have an e-book contract with Palgrave/Macmillan?

	Yes	No
Entire Sample	2.86%	97.14%

Table 5.3: Does your library have an e-book contract with Safari?

	Yes	No
Entire Sample	10.00%	90.00%

Table 5.4: Does your library have an e-book contract with McGraw-Hill eBook Library?

	Yes	No
Entire Sample	10.00%	90.00%

Table 5.5: Does your library have an e-book contract with ABC-CLIO?

	Yes	No
Entire Sample	5.71%	94.29%

Table 5.6: Does your library have an e-book contract with Amazon?

	Yes	No
Entire Sample	2.86%	97.14%

Table 5.7: Does your library have an e-book contract with Baker & Taylor?

	Yes	No
Entire Sample	1.43%	98.57%

Table 5.8: Does your library have an e-book contract with SciVerse Science Direct?

	Yes	No
Entire Sample	15.71%	84.29%

Table 5.9: Does your library have an e-book contract with Ellibs?

	Yes	No
Entire Sample	0.00%	100.00%

Table 5.10: Does your library have an e-book contract with OverDrive?

	Yes	No
Entire Sample	18.57%	81.43%

Table 5.11: Does your library have an e-book contract with Follett Higher Education Group?

	Yes	No
Entire Sample	0.00%	100.00%

Table 5.12: Does your library have an e-book contract with MyiLibrary?

	Yes	No
Entire Sample	10.00%	90.00%

Table 5.13: Does your library have an e-book contract with Ebrary?

	Yes	No
Entire Sample	32.86%	67.14%

Table 5.14: Does your library have an e-book contract with Knovel?

	Yes	No
Entire Sample	8.57%	91.43%

Table 5.15: Does your library have an e-book contract with Lecture Notes in Computer Science?

	Yes	No
Entire Sample	4.29%	95.71%

Table 5.16: Does your library have an e-book contract with EBL?

	Yes	No
Entire Sample	10.00%	90.00%

Table 5.17: Does your library have an e-book contract with Gale Virtual Reference Library?

	Yes	No
Entire Sample	27.14%	72.86%

Table 5.18: Does your library have an e-book contract with Bookish?

	Yes	No
Entire Sample	0.00%	100.00%

Table 5.19: Does your library have an e-book contract with Wiley Online Library?

	Yes	No
Entire Sample	12.86%	87.14%

Table 5.20: Does your library have an e-book contract with SwetsWise?

	Yes	No
Entire Sample	2.86%	97.14%

Table 6: Does the library have a current contract for e-books from any of the following vendors? Broken out by Country

Table 6.1: Does the library have an e-book contract with NetLibrary/EBSCO? Broken out by Country

Country	Yes	No
United States	44.00%	56.00%
Other	30.00%	70.00%

Table 6.2: Does your library have an e-book contract with Palgrave/Macmillan? Broken out by Country

Country	Yes	No
United States	0.00%	100.00%
Other	10.00%	90.00%

Table 6.3: Does your library have an e-book contract with Safari? Broken out by Country

Country	Yes	No
United States	6.00%	94.00%
Other	20.00%	80.00%

Table 6.4: Does your library have an e-book contract with McGraw-Hill eBook Library? Broken out by Country

Country	Yes	No
United States	8.00%	92.00%
Other	15.00%	85.00%

Table 6.5: Does your library have an e-book contract with ABC-CLIO? Broken out by Country

Country	Yes	No
United States	8.00%	92.00%
Other	0.00%	100.00%

Table 6.6: Does your library have an e-book contract with Amazon? Broken out by Country

Country	Yes	No
United States	4.00%	96.00%
Other	0.00%	100.00%

Table 6.7: Does your library have an e-book contract with Baker & Taylor? Broken out by Country

Country	Yes	No
United States	2.00%	98.00%
Other	0.00%	100.00%

Table 6.8: Does your library have an e-book contract with SciVerse Science Direct? Broken out by Country

Country	Yes	No
United States	14.00%	86.00%
Other	20.00%	80.00%

Table 6.9: Does your library have an e-book contract with OverDrive? Broken out by Country

Country	Yes	No
United States	24.00%	76.00%
Other	5.00%	95.00%

Table 6.10: Does your library have an e-book contract with MyiLibrary? Broken out by Country

Country	Yes	No
United States	4.00%	96.00%
Other	25.00%	75.00%

Table 6.11: Does your library have an e-book contract with Ebrary? Broken out by Country

Country	Yes	No
United States	30.00%	70.00%
Other	40.00%	60.00%

Table 6.12: Does your library have an e-book contract with Knovel? Broken out by Country

Country	Yes	No
United States	6.00%	94.00%
Other	15.00%	85.00%

Table 6.13: Does your library have an e-book contract with Lecture Notes in Computer Science? Broken out by Country

Country	Yes	No
United States	0.00%	100.00%
Other	15.00%	85.00%

Table 6.14: Does your library have an e-book contract with EBL? Broken out by Country

Country	Yes	No
United States	8.00%	92.00%
Other	15.00%	85.00%

Table 6.15: Does your library have an e-book contract with Gale Virtual Reference Library? Broken out by Country

Country	Yes	No
United States	34.00%	66.00%
Other	10.00%	90.00%

Table 6.16: Does your library have an e-book contract with Wiley Online Library? Broken out by Country

Country	Yes	No
United States	10.00%	90.00%
Other	20.00%	80.00%

Table 6.17: Does your library have an e-book contract with SwetsWise? Broken out by Country

Country	Yes	No
United States	2.00%	98.00%
Other	5.00%	95.00%

Table 7: Does the library have a current contract for e-books from any of the following vendors? Broken out by Type of Library

Table 7.1: Does the library have an e-book contract with NetLibrary/EBSCO? Broken out by Type of Library

Type of Library	Yes	No
Public Library	10.53%	89.47%
College Library	66.67%	33.33%
Other	22.22%	77.78%

Table 7.2: Does your library have an e-book contract with Palgrave/Macmillan? Broken out by Type of Library

Type of Library	Yes	No
Public Library	0.00%	100.00%
College Library	6.06%	93.94%
Other	0.00%	100.00%

Table 7.3: Does your library have an e-book contract with Safari? Broken out by Type of Library

Type of Library	Yes	No
Public Library	5.26%	94.74%
College Library	15.15%	84.85%
Other	5.56%	94.44%

Table 7.4: Does your library have an e-book contract with McGraw-Hill eBook Library? Broken out by Type of Library

Type of Library	Yes	No
Public Library	0.00%	100.00%
College Library	15.15%	84.85%
Other	11.11%	88.89%

Table 7.5: Does your library have an e-book contract with ABC-CLIO? Broken out by Type of Library

Type of Library	Yes	No
Public Library	0.00%	100.00%
College Library	12.12%	87.88%
Other	0.00%	100.00%

Table 7.6: Does your library have an e-book contract with Amazon? Broken out by Type of Library

Type of Library	Yes	No
Public Library	5.26%	94.74%
College Library	3.03%	96.97%
Other	0.00%	100.00%

Table 7.7: Does your library have an e-book contract with Baker & Taylor? Broken out by Type of Library

Type of Library	Yes	No
Public Library	5.26%	94.74%
College Library	0.00%	100.00%
Other	0.00%	100.00%

Table 7.8: Does your library have an e-book contract with SciVerse Science Direct? Broken out by Type of Library

Type of Library	Yes	No
Public Library	0.00%	100.00%
College Library	27.27%	72.73%
Other	11.11%	88.89%

Table 7.9: Does your library have an e-book contract with OverDrive? Broken out by Type of Library

Type of Library	Yes	No
Public Library	68.42%	31.58%
College Library	0.00%	100.00%
Other	0.00%	100.00%

Table 7.10: Does your library have an e-book contract with MyiLibrary? Broken out by Type of Library

Type of Library	Yes	No
Public Library	0.00%	100.00%
College Library	18.18%	81.82%
Other	5.56%	94.44%

Table 7.11: Does your library have an e-book contract with Ebrary? Broken out by Type of Library

Type of Library	Yes	No
Public Library	0.00%	100.00%
College Library	63.64%	36.36%
Other	11.11%	88.89%

Table 7.12: Does your library have an e-book contract with Knovel? Broken out by Type of Library

Type of Library	Yes	No
Public Library	0.00%	100.00%
College Library	15.15%	84.85%
Other	5.56%	94.44%

Table 7.13: Does your library have an e-book contract with Lecture Notes in Computer Science? Broken out by Type of Library

Type of Library	Yes	No
Public Library	0.00%	100.00%
College Library	6.06%	93.94%
Other	5.56%	94.44%

Table 7.14: Does your library have an e-book contract with EBL? Broken out by Type of Library

Type of Library	Yes	No
Public Library	0.00%	100.00%
College Library	18.18%	81.82%
Other	5.56%	94.44%

Table 7.15: Does your library have an e-book contract with Gale Virtual Reference Library? Broken out by Type of Library

Type of Library	Yes	No
Public Library	15.79%	84.21%
College Library	45.45%	54.55%
Other	5.56%	94.44%

Table 7.16: Does your library have an e-book contract with Wiley Online Library? Broken out by Type of Library

Type of Library	Yes	No
Public Library	0.00%	100.00%
College Library	21.21%	78.79%
Other	11.11%	88.89%

Table 7.17: Does your library have an e-book contract with SwetsWise? Broken out by Type of Library

Type of Library	Yes	No
Public Library	0.00%	100.00%
College Library	6.06%	93.94%
Other	0.00%	100.00%

Table 8: Does the library have a current contract for e-books from any of the following vendors? Broken out by Total Library Budget

Table 8.1: Does the library have an e-book contract with NetLibrary/EBSCO? Broken out by Total Library Budget

Library Budget	Yes	No
Less than $500,000	26.92%	73.08%
$500,000 to $4 Million	50.00%	50.00%
More than $4 Million	44.44%	55.56%

Table 8.2: Does your library have an e-book contract with Palgrave/Macmillan? Broken out by Total Library Budget

Library Budget	Yes	No
Less than $500,000	3.85%	96.15%
$500,000 to $4 Million	0.00%	100.00%
More than $4 Million	5.56%	94.44%

Table 8.3: Does your library have an e-book contract with Safari? Broken out by Total Library Budget

Library Budget	Yes	No
Less than $500,000	0.00%	100.00%
$500,000 to $4 Million	3.85%	96.15%
More than $4 Million	33.33%	66.67%

Table 8.4: Does your library have an e-book contract with McGraw-Hill eBook Library? Broken out by Total Library Budget

Library Budget	Yes	No
Less than $500,000	7.69%	92.31%
$500,000 to $4 Million	7.69%	92.31%
More than $4 Million	16.67%	83.33%

Table 8.5: Does your library have an e-book contract with ABC-CLIO? Broken out by Total Library Budget

Library Budget	Yes	No
Less than $500,000	7.69%	92.31%
$500,000 to $4 Million	7.69%	92.31%
More than $4 Million	0.00%	100.00%

Table 8.6: Does your library have an e-book contract with Amazon? Broken out by Total Library Budget

Library Budget	Yes	No
Less than $500,000	7.69%	92.31%
$500,000 to $4 Million	0.00%	100.00%
More than $4 Million	0.00%	100.00%

Table 8.7: Does your library have an e-book contract with Baker & Taylor? Broken out by Total Library Budget

Library Budget	Yes	No
Less than $500,000	0.00%	100.00%
$500,000 to $4 Million	3.85%	96.15%
More than $4 Million	0.00%	100.00%

Table 8.8: Does your library have an e-book contract with SciVerse Science Direct? Broken out by Total Library Budget

Library Budget	Yes	No
Less than $500,000	0.00%	100.00%
$500,000 to $4 Million	15.38%	84.62%
More than $4 Million	38.89%	61.11%

Table 8.9: Does your library have an e-book contract with OverDrive? Broken out by Total Library Budget

Library Budget	Yes	No
Less than $500,000	11.54%	88.46%
$500,000 to $4 Million	15.38%	84.62%
More than $4 Million	33.33%	66.67%

Table 8.10: Does your library have an e-book contract with MyiLibrary? Broken out by Total Library Budget

Library Budget	Yes	No
Less than $500,000	3.85%	96.15%
$500,000 to $4 Million	7.69%	92.31%
More than $4 Million	22.22%	77.78%

Table 8.11: Does your library have an e-book contract with Ebrary? Broken out by Total Library Budget

Library Budget	Yes	No
Less than $500,000	19.23%	80.77%
$500,000 to $4 Million	34.62%	65.38%
More than $4 Million	50.00%	50.00%

Table 8.12: Does your library have an e-book contract with Knovel? Broken out by Total Library Budget

Library Budget	Yes	No
Less than $500,000	0.00%	100.00%
$500,000 to $4 Million	7.69%	92.31%
More than $4 Million	22.22%	77.78%

Table 8.13: Does your library have an e-book contract with Lecture Notes in Computer Science? Broken out by Total Library Budget

Library Budget	Yes	No
Less than $500,000	0.00%	100.00%
$500,000 to $4 Million	0.00%	100.00%
More than $4 Million	16.67%	83.33%

Table 8.14: Does your library have an e-book contract with EBL? Broken out by Total Library Budget

Library Budget	Yes	No
Less than $500,000	3.85%	96.15%
$500,000 to $4 Million	3.85%	96.15%
More than $4 Million	27.78%	72.22%

Table 8.15: Does your library have an e-book contract with Gale Virtual Reference Library? Broken out by Total Library Budget

Library Budget	Yes	No
Less than $500,000	11.54%	88.46%
$500,000 to $4 Million	26.92%	73.08%
More than $4 Million	50.00%	50.00%

Table 8.16: Does your library have an e-book contract with Wiley Online Library? Broken out by Total Library Budget

Library Budget	Yes	No
Less than $500,000	0.00%	100.00%
$500,000 to $4 Million	11.54%	88.46%
More than $4 Million	33.33%	66.67%

Table 8.17: Does your library have an e-book contract with SwetsWise? Broken out by Total Library Budget

Library Budget	Yes	No
Less than $500,000	0.00%	100.00%
$500,000 to $4 Million	0.00%	100.00%
More than $4 Million	11.11%	88.89%

Table 9.1: How many existing e-book licensing contracts does the library have with individual publishers or aggregators?

	Mean	Median	Minimum	Maximum
Entire Sample	3.92	2.00	0.00	21.00

Table 9.2: How many existing e-book licensing contracts does the library have with individual publishers or aggregators? Broken out by Country

Country	Mean	Median	Minimum	Maximum
United States	3.48	2.00	0.00	17.00
Other	5.00	3.00	0.00	21.00

Table 9.3: How many existing e-book licensing contracts does the library have with individual publishers or aggregators? Broken out by Type of Library

Type of Library	Mean	Median	Minimum	Maximum
Public Library	1.06	1.00	0.00	4.00
College Library	5.97	4.00	0.00	21.00
Other	2.56	1.50	0.00	10.00

Table 9.4: How many existing e-book licensing contracts does the library have with individual publishers or aggregators? Broken out by Total Library Budget

Library Budget	Mean	Median	Minimum	Maximum
Less than $500,000	1.48	1.00	0.00	5.00
$500,000 to $4 Million	4.00	2.00	0.00	15.00
More than $4 Million	6.94	4.00	0.00	21.00

What are a few of your favorite e-book suppliers and why do you like them?

1. In the Italian law sector there are only a few e-book suppliers and so far my library has used only one of them, thus I cannot say which supplier is our favorite
2. Gale Virtual Reference Library – amazing customer service (fast, responsive, open to negotiating)
3. Amazon so far is one of the best, since we can easily add several readers or apps and send material directly. However, there is no one good product yet, not one that solves the needs of an academic or community library.
4. NetLibrary/EBSCO – excellent service, pertinent subject material, one platform for use by USA and international students
5. We only purchase through OverDrive Advantage. We like it as it is the only e-book vendor recommended by the State Library.
6. 3M because it has one of the six publishers that wouldn't play otherwise. OverDrive because it has improved its interface.
7. We are in a consortium with other libraries in the state with a shared collection in OverDrive; this enables more access to e-books for our patrons through the shared collection.
8. We chose OverDrive because it had the best access to bestselling fiction
9. Ebrary – I love the Academic Complete collection and the opportunity to purchase other individual titles.
10. EBSCO and EBL. Users can download e-books and can order directly the books they want consult.
11. Safari
12. Springer and Cambridge University Press. No DRM, very high usage.
13. EBL – more flexibility in delivery, PDA program, and platform is more user friendly. Elsevier – platform mirrors their journals.
14. Safari – allows you to add and drop titles. EBL – PDA with flexibility to change options. Publishers – no DRM, no proprietary reader and mobile apps.
15. OverDrive – Kindle
16. EBSCO Content Manager – ad hoc purchasing, no contract, compatible with our discovery service
17. Amazon is the only one used so far. No contract, purchase as needed.
18. McGraw-Hill, Ovid, R2 because of ease of use
19. Thieme – they provide new books all year long
20. OverDrive – easy to use, great support
21. NetLibrary. Cost savings through Lyrasis.
22. The only one we currently have is OverDrive. They provide many of the titles our customers want.
23. Amazon – low price

24. Elsevier – ease of use. Medical titles appropriate for our clinical staff – there's really not much of a variety of vendors to choose from in this highly specialized area.
25. As a solo librarian, considering EBSCO and YBP for the collection development support available. Also EBSCO various PDA and purchase (rather than subscription) models.
26. Ebrary because there are so many books available and because our students love the Ebrary features such as highlighter pens and bookshelf. Credo Reference because it is a good alternative to Wikipedia and students like the fact that it shows clearly how to reference each item at the bottom of individual entries.
27. R2Library, Thieme E-Book Library, Karger E-Book Library, OVID E-Book Library, MDConsult E-Book Library and PsychiatryOnline E-Book Library – they carry medical books
28. Dawsonera – relevance of material, easy web access
29. Dawsonera platform – credit system allows concurrent access
30. Ebrary – has offered attractive pricing and good support
31. McGraw-Hill – easy to work with and we can also develop customized texts
32. YBP, EBL – good service
33. Rittenhouse R2Library (IP authentication and easy user set up for remote access. Good+ user interface)
34. Lexis/Matthew Bender
35. EBSCO – easy access
36. EBSCI because it's a familiar platform and works with Summon
37. I don't have favorites. We subscribe to three collections of e-books for the content that is provided.
38. Ebrary; I like them because they have such a wide variety of subjects and reading levels for community college students.
39. 3M Cloud Library and Overdrive because they have the best selection of titles for public libraries.
40. EBL offers unlimited simultaneous viewing by users for list price. Gale VRL titles do not have DRM.
41. EBSCO – quality academic books at low cost. Ebrary – quality academic books at low cost.
42. Ebrary via YBP – easy to purchase and use, same with GVRL
43. Springer – no DRM. Ebrary – easy to use interface.
44. Springer unlimited downloads, Ebrary via Yankee interface with discovery platform
45. Ebrary – complete sets
46. Gale. We get to select the titles we want, not get stuck with a package with a lot of stuff we don't want.
47. EBSCO – integrates well with their platform. Cambridge – excellent content.
48. Springer – no DRM, easy for users, content we need, consortia pricing is attractive. Ebrary content has improved a lot over the 4 years we have subscribed to the academic complete collection, though remote and mobile access still tricky.
49. Ebrary – love getting 70,000 titles for such low cost on subscription. MyiLibrary – we have a PDA with them and like the 3 view trigger for a purchase.
50. EBSCO, it is a familiar interface and user friendly

Table 10.1: What percentage of the e-book contracts that your library currently has do you expect to renew upon completion of the current contract?

	Mean	Median	Minimum	Maximum
Entire Sample	74.57%	100.00%	0.00%	100.00%

Table 10.2: What percentage of the e-book contracts that your library currently has do you expect to renew upon completion of the current contract? Broken out by Country

Country	Mean	Median	Minimum	Maximum
United States	68.46%	100.00%	0.00%	100.00%
Other	89.06%	100.00%	0.00%	100.00%

Table 10.3: What percentage of the e-book contracts that your library currently has do you expect to renew upon completion of the current contract? Broken out by Type of Library

Type of Library	Mean	Median	Minimum	Maximum
Public Library	73.46%	100.00%	0.00%	100.00%
College Library	75.88%	100.00%	0.00%	100.00%
Other	73.00%	100.00%	0.00%	100.00%

Table 10.4: What percentage of the e-book contracts that your library currently has do you expect to renew upon completion of the current contract? Broken out by Total Library Budget

Library Budget	Mean	Median	Minimum	Maximum
Less than $500,000	75.34%	100.00%	0.00%	100.00%
$500,000 to $4 Million	66.40%	100.00%	0.00%	100.00%
More than $4 Million	83.41%	100.00%	0.90%	100.00%

Table 11: How much did your library spend in the past year on e-books or e-documents from the following vendors in the past year?

Table 11.1: How much did your library spend on e-books from Amazon in the past year? (in $US)

	Mean	Median	Minimum	Maximum
Entire Sample	$357.97	$0.00	$0.00	$20,000.00

Table 11.2: How much did your library spend on e-books from Barnes & Noble in the past year? (in $US)

	Mean	Median	Minimum	Maximum
Entire Sample	$475.74	$0.00	$0.00	$20,000.00

Table 11.3: How much did your library spend on e-books from Google in the past year? (in $US)

	Mean	Median	Minimum	Maximum
Entire Sample	$0.77	$0.00	$0.00	$50.00

Table 11.4: How much did your library spend on e-books from other online book vendors in the past year? (in $US)

	Mean	Median	Minimum	Maximum
Entire Sample	$11,744.37	$0.00	$0.00	$216,093.00

Table 12: How much did your library spend in the past year on e-books or e-documents from the following vendors in the past year? Broken out by Country

Table 12.1: How much did your library spend on e-books from Amazon? Broken out by Country (in $US)

Country	Mean	Median	Minimum	Maximum
United States	$84.69	$0.00	$0.00	$2,500.00
Other	$1,027.50	$0.00	$0.00	$20,000.00

Table 12.2: How much did your library spend on e-books from Barnes & Noble? Broken out by Country (in $US)

Country	Mean	Median	Minimum	Maximum
United States	$48.96	$0.00	$0.00	$2,000.00
Other	$1,500.00	$0.00	$0.00	$20,000.00

Table 12.3: How much did your library spend on e-books from Google? Broken out by Country (in $US)

Country	Mean	Median	Minimum	Maximum
United States	$0.00	$0.00	$0.00	$0.00
Other	$2.63	$0.00	$0.00	$50.00

Table 12.4: How much did your library spend on e-books from other online book vendors in the past year? Broken out by Country (in $US)

Country	Mean	Median	Minimum	Maximum
United States	$7,697.43	$0.00	$0.00	$200,000.00
Other	$21,116.21	$0.00	$0.00	$216,093.00

Table 13: How much did your library spend in the past year on e-books or e-documents from the following vendors in the past year? Broken out by Type of Library

Table 13.1: How much did your library spend on e-books from Amazon? Broken out by Type of Library (in $US)

Type of Library	Mean	Median	Minimum	Maximum
Public Library	$15.79	$0.00	$0.00	$300.00
College Library	$40.63	$0.00	$0.00	$500.00
Other	$1,283.33	$0.00	$0.00	$20,000.00

Table 13.2: How much did your library spend on e-books from Barnes & Noble? Broken out by Type of Library (in $US)

Type of Library	Mean	Median	Minimum	Maximum
Public Library	$115.79	$0.00	$0.00	$2,000.00
College Library	$327.42	$0.00	$0.00	$10,000.00
Other	$1,111.11	$0.00	$0.00	$20,000.00

Table 13.3: How much did your library spend on e-books from Google? Broken out by Type of Library (in $US)

Type of Library	Mean	Median	Minimum	Maximum
Public Library	$0.00	$0.00	$0.00	$0.00
College Library	$0.00	$0.00	$0.00	$0.00
Other	$2.94	$0.00	$0.00	$50.00

Table 13.4: How much did your library spend on e-books from other online book vendors in the past year? Broken out by Type of Library (in $US)

Type of Library	Mean	Median	Minimum	Maximum
Public Library	$12,340.76	$0.00	$0.00	$200,000.00
College Library	$12,805.07	$0.00	$0.00	$216,093.00
Other	$9,338.53	$0.00	$0.00	$132,234.00

Table 14: How much did your library spend in the past year on e-books or e-documents from the following vendors in the past year? Broken out by Total Library Budget

Table 14.1: How much did your library spend on e-books from Amazon? Broken out by Total Library Budget (in $US)

Library Budget	Mean	Median	Minimum	Maximum
Less than $500,000	$148.08	$0.00	$0.00	$2,500.00
$500,000 to $4 Million	$822.00	$0.00	$0.00	$20,000.00
More than $4 Million	$16.67	$0.00	$0.00	$300.00

Table 14.2: How much did your library spend on e-books from Barnes & Noble? Broken out by Total Library Budget (in $US)

Library Budget	Mean	Median	Minimum	Maximum
Less than $500,000	$392.31	$0.00	$0.00	$10,000.00
$500,000 to $4 Million	$916.67	$0.00	$0.00	$20,000.00
More than $4 Million	$8.33	$0.00	$0.00	$150.00

Table 14.3: How much did your library spend on e-books from Google? Broken out by Total Library Budget (in $US)

Library Budget	Mean	Median	Minimum	Maximum
Less than $500,000	$0.00	$0.00	$0.00	$0.00
$500,000 to $4 Million	$2.27	$0.00	$0.00	$50.00
More than $4 Million	$0.00	$0.00	$0.00	$0.00

Table 14.4: How much did your library spend on e-books from other online book vendors in the past year? Broken out by Total Library Budget (in $US)

Library Budget	Mean	Median	Minimum	Maximum
Less than $500,000	$2,413.60	$0.00	$0.00	$37,000.00
$500,000 to $4 Million	$3,278.57	$0.00	$0.00	$38,000.00
More than $4 Million	$35,923.82	$0.00	$0.00	$216,093.00

CHAPTER 2: E-BOOK DISTRIBUTION

Table 15: What percentage of the library's total spending on e-books was with the following type of vendor?

Table 15.1: What percentage of the library's total e-book spending was with aggregators?

	Mean	Median	Minimum	Maximum
Entire Sample	79.06%	98.00%	0.00%	100.00%

Table 15.2: What percentage of the library's total e-book spending was with individual publishers?

	Mean	Median	Minimum	Maximum
Entire Sample	20.94%	2.00%	0.00%	100.00%

Table 16: What percentage of the library's total spending on e-books was with the following type of vendor? Broken out by Country

Table 16.1: What percentage of the library's total e-book spending was with aggregators? Broken out by Country

Country	Mean	Median	Minimum	Maximum
United States	82.49%	100.00%	0.00%	100.00%
Other	72.39%	90.00%	0.00%	100.00%

Table 16.2: What percentage of the library's total e-book spending was with individual publishers? Broken out by Country

Country	Mean	Median	Minimum	Maximum
United States	17.51%	0.00%	0.00%	100.00%
Other	27.61%	10.00%	0.00%	100.00%

Table 17: What percentage of the library's total spending on e-books was with the following type of vendor? Broken out by Type of Library

Table 17.1: What percentage of the library's total e-book spending was with aggregators? Broken out by Type of Library

Type of Library	Mean	Median	Minimum	Maximum
Public Library	99.85%	100.00%	98.00%	100.00%
College Library	74.23%	87.50%	0.00%	100.00%
Other	68.71%	92.50%	0.00%	100.00%

Table 17.2: What percentage of the library's total e-book spending was with individual publishers? Broken out by Type of Library

Type of Library	Mean	Median	Minimum	Maximum
Public Library	0.15%	0.00%	0.00%	2.00%
College Library	25.77%	12.50%	0.00%	100.00%
Other	31.29%	7.50%	0.00%	100.00%

Table 18: What percentage of the library's total spending on e-books was with the following type of vendor? Broken out by Total Library Budget

Table 18.1: What percentage of the library's total e-book spending was with aggregators? Broken out by Total Library Budget

Library Budget	Mean	Median	Minimum	Maximum
Less than $500,000	74.00%	95.00%	0.00%	100.00%
$500,000 to $4 Million	85.00%	99.00%	0.00%	100.00%
More than $4 Million	75.63%	94.00%	5.00%	100.00%

Table 18.2: What percentage of the library's total e-book spending was with individual publishers? Broken out by Total Library Budget

Library Budget	Mean	Median	Minimum	Maximum
Less than $500,000	26.00%	5.00%	0.00%	100.00%
$500,000 to $4 Million	15.00%	1.00%	0.00%	100.00%
More than $4 Million	24.38%	6.00%	0.00%	95.00%

Table 19: What percentage of the number of separate e-book contracts (not their value or size) does the library have with each specific type of vendor?

Table 19.1: What percentage of total e-book contracts does the library have with aggregators?

	Mean	Median	Minimum	Maximum
Entire Sample	75.42%	99.00%	0.00%	100.00%

Table 19.2: What percentage of total e-book contracts does the library have with individual publishers?

	Mean	Median	Minimum	Maximum
Entire Sample	24.58%	1.00%	0.00%	100.00%

Table 20: What percentage of the number of separate e-book contracts (not their value or size) does the library have with each specific type of vendor? Broken out by Country

Table 20.1: What percentage of total e-book contracts does the library have with aggregators? Broken out by Country

Country	Mean	Median	Minimum	Maximum
United States	81.29%	100.00%	0.00%	100.00%
Other	62.43%	90.00%	0.00%	100.00%

Table 20.2: What percentage of total e-book contracts does the library have with individual publishers? Broken out by Country

Country	Mean	Median	Minimum	Maximum
United States	18.71%	0.00%	0.00%	100.00%
Other	37.57%	10.00%	0.00%	100.00%

Table 21: What percentage of the number of separate e-book contracts (not their value or size) does the library have with each specific type of vendor? Broken out by Type of Library

Table 21.1: What percentage of total e-book contracts does the library have with aggregators? Broken out by Type of Library

Type of Library	Mean	Median	Minimum	Maximum
Public Library	98.08%	100.00%	75.00%	100.00%
College Library	72.55%	90.00%	20.00%	100.00%
Other	52.30%	57.50%	0.00%	100.00%

Table 21.2: What percentage of total e-book contracts does the library have with individual publishers? Broken out by Type of Library

Type of Library	Mean	Median	Minimum	Maximum
Public Library	1.92%	0.00%	0.00%	25.00%
College Library	27.45%	10.00%	0.00%	80.00%
Other	47.70%	42.50%	0.00%	100.00%

Table 22: What percentage of the number of separate e-book contracts (not their value or size) does the library have with each specific type of vendor? Broken out by Total Library Budget

Table 22.1: What percentage of total e-book contracts does the library have with aggregators? Broken out by Total Library Budget

Library Budget	Mean	Median	Minimum	Maximum
Less than $500,000	75.71%	92.50%	0.00%	100.00%
$500,000 to $4 Million	79.76%	100.00%	10.00%	100.00%
More than $4 Million	69.86%	95.00%	0.00%	100.00%

Table 22.2: What percentage of total e-book contracts does the library have with individual publishers? Broken out by Total Library Budget

Library Budget	Mean	Median	Minimum	Maximum
Less than $500,000	24.29%	7.50%	0.00%	100.00%
$500,000 to $4 Million	20.24%	0.00%	0.00%	90.00%
More than $4 Million	30.14%	5.00%	0.00%	100.00%

Table 23: What percentage of the library's total e-book ordering was made through the following channels?

Table 23.1: What percentage of e-book ordering was made through e-book divisions of a traditional book jobber or distributor?

	Mean	Median	Minimum	Maximum
Entire Sample	37.13%	10.00%	0.00%	100.00%

Table 23.2: What percentage of e-book ordering was made through an electronic information aggregator not connected to a major book jobber or distributor?

	Mean	Median	Minimum	Maximum
Entire Sample	46.44%	41.50%	0.00%	100.00%

Table 23.3: What percentage of e-book ordering made directly from a publisher?

	Mean	Median	Minimum	Maximum
Entire Sample	16.42%	0.00%	0.00%	100.00%

Table 24: What percentage of the library's total e-book ordering was made through the following channels? Broken out by Country

Table 24.1: What percentage of e-book ordering was made through e-book divisions of a traditional book jobber or distributor?

Country	Mean	Median	Minimum	Maximum
United States	35.72%	10.00%	0.00%	100.00%
Other	40.31%	12.50%	0.00%	100.00%

Table 24.2: What percentage of e-book ordering was made through an electronic information aggregator not connected to a major book jobber or distributor?

Country	Mean	Median	Minimum	Maximum
United States	50.75%	51.50%	0.00%	100.00%
Other	36.75%	7.50%	0.00%	100.00%

Table 24.3: What percentage of e-book ordering made directly from a publisher?

Country	Mean	Median	Minimum	Maximum
United States	13.53%	0.00%	0.00%	100.00%
Other	22.94%	5.00%	0.00%	100.00%

Table 25: What percentage of the library's total e-book ordering was made through the following channels? Broken out by Type of Library

Table 25.1: What percentage of e-book ordering was made through e-book divisions of a traditional book jobber or distributor?

Type of Library	Mean	Median	Minimum	Maximum
Public Library	14.64%	0.00%	0.00%	100.00%
College Library	52.44%	50.00%	0.00%	100.00%
Other	31.92%	0.00%	0.00%	100.00%

Table 25.2: What percentage of e-book ordering was made through an electronic information aggregator not connected to a major book jobber or distributor?

Type of Library	Mean	Median	Minimum	Maximum
Public Library	85.21%	100.00%	0.00%	100.00%
College Library	33.60%	15.00%	0.00%	100.00%
Other	29.38%	5.00%	0.00%	100.00%

Table 25.3: What percentage of e-book ordering made directly from a publisher?

Type of Library	Mean	Median	Minimum	Maximum
Public Library	0.14%	0.00%	0.00%	2.00%
College Library	13.96%	2.00%	0.00%	80.00%
Other	38.69%	5.00%	0.00%	100.00%

Table 26: What percentage of the library's total e-book ordering was made through the following channels? Broken out by Total Library Budget

Table 26.1: What percentage of e-book ordering was made through e-book divisions of a traditional book jobber or distributor?

Library Budget	Mean	Median	Minimum	Maximum
Less than $500,000	51.67%	75.00%	0.00%	100.00%
$500,000 to $4 Million	37.52%	0.00%	0.00%	100.00%
More than $4 Million	23.00%	5.00%	0.00%	100.00%

Table 26.2: What percentage of e-book ordering was made through an electronic information aggregator not connected to a major book jobber or distributor?

Library Budget	Mean	Median	Minimum	Maximum
Less than $500,000	31.33%	0.00%	0.00%	100.00%
$500,000 to $4 Million	47.48%	20.00%	0.00%	100.00%
More than $4 Million	59.25%	61.50%	0.00%	100.00%

Table 26.3: What percentage of e-book ordering made directly from a publisher?

Library Budget	Mean	Median	Minimum	Maximum
Less than $500,000	17.00%	0.00%	0.00%	100.00%
$500,000 to $4 Million	15.00%	0.00%	0.00%	100.00%
More than $4 Million	17.75%	1.00%	0.00%	90.00%

Table 27.1: What percentage of the library's e-book collection spending is through contracts negotiated by consortium?

	Mean	Median	Minimum	Maximum
Entire Sample	29.83%	0.00%	0.00%	100.00%

Table 27.2: What percentage of the library's e-book collection spending is through contracts negotiated by consortium? Broken out by Country

Country	Mean	Median	Minimum	Maximum
United States	29.76%	0.00%	0.00%	100.00%
Other	30.00%	0.00%	0.00%	100.00%

Table 27.3: What percentage of the library's e-book collection spending is through contracts negotiated by consortium? Broken out by Type of Library

Type of Library	Mean	Median	Minimum	Maximum
Public Library	31.76%	0.00%	0.00%	100.00%
College Library	35.13%	12.00%	0.00%	100.00%
Other	18.89%	0.00%	0.00%	100.00%

Table 27.4: What percentage of the library's e-book collection spending is through contracts negotiated by consortium? Broken out by Total Library Budget

Library Budget	Mean	Median	Minimum	Maximum
Less than $500,000	26.67%	0.00%	0.00%	100.00%
$500,000 to $4 Million	31.11%	6.00%	0.00%	100.00%
More than $4 Million	32.50%	7.50%	0.00%	100.00%

What provisions have you made to help your patrons to find and download or otherwise utilize the many e-books in the public domain that are now available?

1. In the catalog a small part of our rare books collection has a link to an online version (i.e. on Google Books). A few other books have a link to the index if it's available online.
2. Links to DOAJ, Project Gutenberg, HathiTrust, National Academies Press. In LibGuides.
3. Post links to these resources, highlight them during instruction or training sessions, and suggest them to those looking for resources
4. When staff is asked we try to assist. No marketing of these public domain resources.
5. We pass out bookmarks with the URL on them, we also tell patrons where to look
6. Two classes offered in January/February of each year to train the new e-readers
7. Have some links on our website and also use the public domain books through OverDrive
8. We currently have directions to use Project Gutenberg on our website
9. Links on our web site; direct recommendation to patrons by staff.
10. We have a list of links that are found on our website to free online books. We continue to seek these out and to keep the list of links up to date.
11. through one on one interactions
12. I can point them to the sources of free e-books but they have to find what they want within those sources
13. Linked from website with instructions
14. We put the information on the website of the library and provide training directly to users
15. links to Google Books
16. I am collection information on sources, and use them when searching for reference work, and pass on source information in conjunction with results where applicable.
17. We have actively and are actively adding catalog records to our ILS with web links.
18. Titles in the public domain are retrievable from our discovery service
19. Website, OPAC, fliers, blog entries and more.
20. While we don't subscribe to e-books, we do provide access to e-content from Lexis/Westlaw/Bloomberg in the catalog. Many of these materials are databases rather than in an e-book format. We also have purchased the digital copies to historic materials through Making of Modern Law and ECCO. These materials are all included in the catalog as well as the database link is on our webpage. We also link to Google Books and teach this resource as well as other free legal resources in our first year classes and upper level classes.
21. Incorporated with discovery service and records in library catalogue

22. Links on the library page. Key titles catalogued.
23. Training frontline staff, informing them through emails & links
24. Links on our website, highlighting them on our website.
25. weekly classes on e-reader devices, web advertising, email newsletters, word of mouth
26. Enter item in catalog - users can see the item in our catalog, and the IP-authenticated link allows them access if they're on a computer within our institution walls.
27. We include links in our online catalog and send them to patrons if they request the title specifically.
28. Customer training, staff training, links on our e-books page
29. Some are now on our catalogue
30. Word of mouth, Facebook, website, newspaper articles
31. purchased a "Discovery service" catalog relevant subject specific books in local OPAC created e-book LibGuide with links to free platforms
32. Dawsonera books individually catalogued and accessible via web catalogue using e-library authentication. T&F e-books available through e-library
33. workshops, LibGuides
34. Post links on the library website train educators (who, in turn, train other staff)
35. training sessions and intranet portal access
36. Library orientation; one-on-one training, pamphlets for specific databases; emails to patrons,
37. link to them from website
38. add MARC records to our online catalog
39. Those available through the state library and archives we link on our website
40. List them in the online catalog.
41. We have links on library webpages for collections of public domain titles, we use Primo Central, and we add MARC records in our catalogue
42. MARC records in catalog, links to databases. Currently creating a special tab containing all e-books.
43. Load all the MARC records of all the e-books in our library catalog or discovery system.
44. Topic Guide Course Guides
45. I conduct one-shot sessions, also there are help sheets available for our users
46. provided links
47. Created a LibGuide on finding e-readers and e-books, including free books.
48. working on this, mostly catalog links
49. some Project Gutenberg MARC records in catalog
50. We occasionally link to HathiTrust of Google books for titles we have withdrawn. Our user guide for e-books includes free resources. Federal documents are primarily added in e-format.
51. online instructions, in library instruction

CHAPTER 3: E-AUDIO BOOKS

Table 28: What was or will be the library's total spending on e-audio books in the following years?

Table 28.1: What was the library's total spending on e-audio books in 2012? (in $US)

	Mean	Median	Minimum	Maximum
Entire Sample	$2,349.52	$0.00	$0.00	$50,000.00

Table 28.2: What was the library's total spending on e-audio books In 2013? (in $US)

	Mean	Median	Minimum	Maximum
Entire Sample	$2,437.53	$0.00	$0.00	$50,000.00

Table 29: What was or will be the library's total spending on e-audio books in the following years? Broken out by Country

Table 29.1: What was the library's total spending on e-audio books in 2012? Broken out by Country (in $US)

Country	Mean	Median	Minimum	Maximum
United States	$3,148.84	$0.00	$0.00	$50,000.00
Other	$540.53	$0.00	$0.00	$7,270.00

Table 29.2: What was the library's total spending on e-audio books in 2013? Broken out by Country (in $US)

Country	Mean	Median	Minimum	Maximum
United States	$3,154.65	$0.00	$0.00	$50,000.00
Other	$814.58	$0.00	$0.00	$7,270.00

Table 30: What was or will be the library's total spending on e-audio books in the following years? Broken out by Type of Library

Table 30.1: What was the library's total spending on e-audio books in 2012? Broken out by Type of Library (in $US)

Type of Library	Mean	Median	Minimum	Maximum
Public Library	$9,969.29	$650.00	$0.00	$50,000.00
College Library	$200.00	$0.00	$0.00	$3,000.00
Other	$5.56	$0.00	$0.00	$100.00

Table 30.2: What was the library's total spending on e-audio books in 2013? Broken out by Type of Library (in $US)

Type of Library	Mean	Median	Minimum	Maximum
Public Library	$9,905.00	$700.00	$0.00	$50,000.00
College Library	$406.73	$0.00	$0.00	$5,000.00
Other	$14.17	$0.00	$0.00	$250.00

Table 31: What was or will be the library's total spending on e-audio books in the following years? Broken out by Total Library Budget

Table 31.1: What was the library's total spending on e-audio books in 2012? Broken out by Total Library Budget (in $US)

Library Budget	Mean	Median	Minimum	Maximum
Less than $500,000	$290.91	$0.00	$0.00	$3,000.00
$500,000 to $4 Million	$2,384.62	$0.00	$0.00	$50,000.00
More than $4 Million	$5,519.29	$0.00	$0.00	$50,000.00

Table 31.2: What was the library's total spending on e-audio books in 2013? Broken out by Total Library Budget (in $US)

Library Budget	Mean	Median	Minimum	Maximum
Less than $500,000	$538.86	$0.00	$0.00	$5,000.00
$500,000 to $4 Million	$2,384.62	$0.00	$0.00	$50,000.00
More than $4 Million	$5,519.43	$0.00	$0.00	$50,000.00

Table 32.1: What is the number of e-audio book titles currently offered by your library?

	Mean	Median	Minimum	Maximum
Entire Sample	1,091.13	0.00	0.00	30,000.00

Table 32.2: What is the number of e-audio book titles currently offered by your library? Broken out by Country

Country	Mean	Median	Minimum	Maximum
United States	1,571.05	0.00	0.00	30,000.00
Other	30.26	0.00	0.00	250.00

Table 32.3: What is the number of e-audio book titles currently offered by your library? Broken out by Type of Library

Type of Library	Mean	Median	Minimum	Maximum
Public Library	4,589.57	407.50	0.00	30,000.00
College Library	79.31	0.00	0.00	1,100.00
Other	0.28	0.00	0.00	5.00

Table 32.4: What is the number of e-audio book titles currently offered by your library? Broken out by Total Library Budget

Library Budget	Mean	Median	Minimum	Maximum
Less than $500,000	206.19	0.00	0.00	4,000.00
$500,000 to $4 Million	1,450.85	0.00	0.00	30,000.00
More than $4 Million	1,750.50	0.00	0.00	10,000.00

Table 33.1: If your library currently offers e-audio book titles, by what percentage will the number of e-audio books offered by the library change over the next year?

	Mean	Median	Minimum	Maximum
Entire Sample	4.83%	0.00%	0.00%	100.00%

Table 33.2: If your library currently offers e-audio book titles, by what percentage will the number of e-audio books offered by the library change over the next year? Broken out by Country

Country	Mean	Median	Minimum	Maximum
United States	5.56%	0.00%	0.00%	100.00%
Other	2.50%	0.00%	0.00%	20.00%

Table 33.3: If your library currently offers e-audio book titles, by what percentage will the number of e-audio books offered by the library change over the next year? Broken out by Type of Library

Type of Library	Mean	Median	Minimum	Maximum
Public Library	5.25%	1.50%	0.00%	20.00%
College Library	1.90%	0.00%	0.00%	20.00%
Other	11.11%	0.00%	0.00%	100.00%

Table 33.4: If your library currently offers e-audio book titles, by what percentage will the number of e-audio books offered by the library change over the next year? Broken out by Total Library Budget

Library Budget	Mean	Median	Minimum	Maximum
Less than $500,000	8.53%	0.00%	0.00%	100.00%
$500,000 to $4 Million	2.33%	0.00%	0.00%	10.00%
More than $4 Million	2.30%	0.00%	0.00%	15.00%

CHAPTER 4: E-BOOKS IN INTERLIBRARY LOAN

Table 34.1: Has the library ever used e-book rental or e-book interlibrary loan sites which enable patrons to have access to an e-book for a fee for a brief specified time period, often 30-60 days?

	Yes	No
Entire Sample	3.17%	96.83%

Table 34.2: Has the library ever used e-book rental or e-book interlibrary loan sites which enable patrons to have access to an e-book for a fee for a brief specified time period, often 30-60 days? Broken out by Country

Country	Yes	No
United States	2.27%	97.73%
Other	5.26%	94.74%

Table 34.3: Has the library ever used e-book rental or e-book interlibrary loan sites which enable patrons to have access to an e-book for a fee for a brief specified time period, often 30-60 days? Broken out by Type of Library

Type of Library	Yes	No
Public Library	0.00%	100.00%
College Library	6.45%	93.55%
Other	0.00%	100.00%

Table 34.4: Has the library ever used e-book rental or e-book interlibrary loan sites which enable patrons to have access to an e-book for a fee for a brief specified time period, often 30-60 days? Broken out by Total Library Budget

Library Budget	Yes	No
Less than $500,000	4.76%	95.24%
$500,000 to $4 Million	0.00%	100.00%
More than $4 Million	6.25%	93.75%

Table 35.1: How much did the library spend exclusively on "borrowing rights" to e-books defined as any model that compels you to pay per time borrowed? (in $US)

	Mean	Median	Minimum	Maximum
Entire Sample	$1,061.98	$0.00	$0.00	$50,000.00

Table 35.2: How much did the library spend exclusively on "borrowing rights" to e-books defined as any model compels you to pay per time borrowed? Broken out by Country (in $US)

Country	Mean	Median	Minimum	Maximum
United States	$15.32	$0.00	$0.00	$320.00
Other	$2,970.59	$0.00	$0.00	$50,000.00

Table 35.3: How much did the library spend exclusively on "borrowing rights" to e-books defined as any model compels you to pay per time borrowed? Broken out by Type of Library (in $US)

Type of Library	Mean	Median	Minimum	Maximum
Public Library	$13.64	$0.00	$0.00	$150.00
College Library	$2,420.24	$0.00	$0.00	$50,000.00
Other	$0.00	$0.00	$0.00	$0.00

Table 35.4: How much did the library spend exclusively on "borrowing rights" to e-books defined as any model compels you to pay per time borrowed? Broken out by Total Library Budget (in $US)

Library Budget	Mean	Median	Minimum	Maximum
Less than $500,000	$26.32	$0.00	$0.00	$500.00
$500,000 to $4 Million	$0.00	$0.00	$0.00	$0.00
More than $4 Million	$4,588.64	$0.00	$0.00	$50,000.00

Table 36.1: Do you think that you might be interested in this kind of site?

	Yes	No
Entire Sample	46.67%	53.33%

Table 36.2: Do you think that you might be interested in this kind of site? Broken out by Country

Country	Yes	No
United States	45.24%	54.76%
Other	50.00%	50.00%

Table 36.3: Do you think that you might be interested in this kind of site? Broken out by Type of Library

Type of Library	Yes	No
Public Library	28.57%	71.43%
College Library	62.07%	37.93%
Other	35.29%	64.71%

Table 36.4: Do you think that you might be interested in this kind of site? Broken out by Total Library Budget

Library Budget	Yes	No
Less than $500,000	45.00%	55.00%
$500,000 to $4 Million	48.00%	52.00%
More than $4 Million	46.67%	53.33%

CHAPTER 5: WHO USES WHAT

Table 37.1: What percentage of the top 20 titles loaned out to patrons in the last year are also available for loan in e-book format?

	Mean	Median	Minimum	Maximum
Entire Sample	12.85%	0.50%	0.00%	100.00%

Table 37.2: What percentage of the top 20 titles loaned out to patrons in the last year are also available for loan in e-book format? Broken out by Country

Country	Mean	Median	Minimum	Maximum
United States	15.12%	0.00%	0.00%	100.00%
Other	7.36%	1.50%	0.00%	50.00%

Table 37.3: What percentage of the top 20 titles loaned out to patrons in the last year are also available for loan in e-book format? Broken out by Type of Library

Type of Library	Mean	Median	Minimum	Maximum
Public Library	29.50%	15.00%	0.00%	95.00%
College Library	6.96%	0.00%	0.00%	100.00%
Other	10.80%	2.00%	0.00%	50.00%

Table 37.4: What percentage of the top 20 titles loaned out to patrons in the last year are also available for loan in e-book format? Broken out by Total Library Budget

Library Budget	Mean	Median	Minimum	Maximum
Less than $500,000	12.58%	2.00%	0.00%	90.00%
$500,000 to $4 Million	7.35%	0.00%	0.00%	50.00%
More than $4 Million	25.67%	5.00%	0.00%	100.00%

In what areas is your library most anxious to build its e-book collection?

1. Reference
2. There is a much higher demand for popular titles that are for leisure reading (as opposed to those for academic purposes). Our collection of popular e-books is very tiny and is likely to expand.
3. Security Studies, Counter Terrorism
4. Bestsellers
5. Our patrons seem to really want popular titles, in both Fiction and Nonfiction
6. All
7. Bestselling Fiction
8. Fiction, Bestsellers
9. Popular fiction
10. General Education, Medicine, Dentistry, Criminal Justice
11. Popular Fiction
12. Social Sciences, Economics, Political Studies, History, Architecture, Business, Medical Sciences, Law, Literature
13. Energy, Encyclopedia
14. MTS
15. Health, Exercise, Computing, Education, History, Business, and Sociology
16. Textbooks
17. Popular Reading and Children's Literature
18. I think we are hesitant to put our toes into the e-book waters as the legal publishers have not had a good, workable plan for a library version of e-books. I know that is changing in the coming year and we will be paying close attention to areas in Domestic and International Law
19. Politics, Government, International Relations
20. Textbooks
21. Neurology
22. Bestsellers, Mysteries
23. Nursing at a reasonable cost
24. Nonfiction
25. Medical titles suitable for physicians and other health care providers addressing topics relating to patient care
26. Leadership, Teamwork, Adult Education, Communication Skills, Process/Quality Improvement in Healthcare
27. Computer Science, Business
28. Politics, Sociology, Journalism, History, Business
29. Medicine, Health, all areas of Biomedicine and Life Sciences
30. Textbooks
31. Health and Education would be our main growth areas for e-books
32. Nursing & Health Sciences, Education
33. Textbooks
34. Engineering and the Sciences
35. Nursing Certification
36. Rule books, Codes
37. Educational, Academic, EFL
38. Cross disciplinary
39. Chemistry, Chemical Engineering, Petrochemicals, Environmental Engineering, Health & Safety
40. Funeral Service

41. Social Sciences, Humanities, Science and Technology
42. Bible/Theology
43. Scholarly Journals & Writings
44. Nursing
45. Computers, Surveying, Automotive, Construction, Welding, etc.
46. Theological Reference
47. All areas
48. Curriculum-related

CHAPTER 6: E-BOOK READERS

Table 38.1: Does the library own a stand-alone e-book reading device of any kind?

	Yes	No
Entire Sample	50.00%	50.00%

Table 38.2: Does the library own a stand-alone e-book reading device of any kind? Broken out by Country

Country	Yes	No
United States	52.38%	47.62%
Other	44.44%	55.56%

Table 38.3: Does the library own a stand-alone e-book reading device of any kind? Broken out by Type of Library

Type of Library	Yes	No
Public Library	71.43%	28.57%
College Library	51.72%	48.28%
Other	29.41%	70.59%

Table 38.4: Does the library own a stand-alone e-book reading device of any kind? Broken out by Total Library Budget

Library Budget	Yes	No
Less than $500,000	40.00%	60.00%
$500,000 to $4 Million	56.00%	44.00%
More than $4 Million	53.33%	46.67%

Table 39: Does the library currently own or lease any of the following to provide e-books to patrons or staff?

Table 39.1: Does the library currently own or lease an Amazon Kindle E-Book Reader?

	Yes	No
Entire Sample	19.12%	80.88%

Table 39.2: Does the library currently own or lease a Sony Reader?

	Yes	No
Entire Sample	11.76%	88.24%

Table 39.3: Does the library currently own or lease an Apple iPad?

	Yes	No
Entire Sample	20.59%	79.41%

Table 39.4: Does the library currently own or lease a Samsung Galaxy?

	Yes	No
Entire Sample	1.47%	98.53%

Table 39.5: Does the library currently own or lease a BlackBerry PlayBook?

	Yes	No
Entire Sample	0.00%	100.00%

Table 39.6: Does the library currently own or lease a Motorola Xoom?

	Yes	No
Entire Sample	0.00%	100.00%

Table 39.7: Does the library currently own or lease a Franklin eBookMan?

	Yes	No
Entire Sample	0.00%	100.00%

Table 39.8: Does the library currently own or lease a Barnes & Noble Nook?

	Yes	No
Entire Sample	13.24%	86.76%

Table 40: Does the library currently own or lease any of the following to provide e-books to patrons or staff? Broken out by Country

Table 40.1: Does the library currently own or lease an Amazon Kindle E-Book Reader? Broken out by Country

Country	Yes	No
United States	22.45%	77.55%
Other	10.53%	89.47%

Table 40.2: Does the library currently own or lease a Sony Reader? Broken out by Country

Country	Yes	No
United States	8.16%	91.84%
Other	21.05%	78.95%

Table 40.3: Does the library currently own or lease an Apple iPad? Broken out by Country

Country	Yes	No
United States	20.41%	79.59%
Other	21.05%	78.95%

Table 40.4: Does the library currently own or lease a Samsung Galaxy? Broken out by Country

Country	Yes	No
United States	2.04%	97.96%
Other	0.00%	100.00%

Table 40.5: Does the library currently own or lease a Barnes & Noble Nook? Broken out by Country

Country	Yes	No
United States	14.29%	85.71%
Other	10.53%	89.47%

Table 41: Does the library currently own or lease any of the following to provide e-books to patrons or staff? Broken out by Type of Library

Table 41.1: Does the library currently own or lease an Amazon Kindle E-Book Reader? Broken out by Type of Library

Type of Library	Yes	No
Public Library	31.58%	68.42%
College Library	12.50%	87.50%
Other	17.65%	82.35%

Table 41.2: Does the library currently own or lease a Sony Reader? Broken out by Type of Library

Type of Library	Yes	No
Public Library	15.79%	84.21%
College Library	12.50%	87.50%
Other	5.88%	94.12%

Table 41.3: Does the library currently own or lease an Apple iPad? Broken out by Type of Library

Type of Library	Yes	No
Public Library	5.26%	94.74%
College Library	25.00%	75.00%
Other	29.41%	70.59%

Table 41.4: Does the library currently own or lease a Samsung Galaxy? Broken out by Type of Library

Type of Library	Yes	No
Public Library	5.26%	94.74%
College Library	0.00%	100.00%
Other	0.00%	100.00%

Table 41.5: Does the library currently own or lease a Barnes & Noble Nook? Broken out by Type of Library

Type of Library	Yes	No
Public Library	26.32%	73.68%
College Library	12.50%	87.50%
Other	0.00%	100.00%

Table 42: Does the library currently own or lease any of the following to provide e-books to patrons or staff? Broken out by Total Library Budget

Table 42.1: Does the library currently own or lease an Amazon Kindle E-Book Reader? Broken out by Total Library Budget

Library Budget	Yes	No
Less than $500,000	24.00%	76.00%
$500,000 to $4 Million	19.23%	80.77%
More than $4 Million	11.76%	88.24%

Table 42.2: Does the library currently own or lease a Sony Reader? Broken out by Total Library Budget

Library Budget	Yes	No
Less than $500,000	12.00%	88.00%
$500,000 to $4 Million	7.69%	92.31%
More than $4 Million	17.65%	82.35%

Table 42.3: Does the library currently own or lease an Apple iPad Broken out by Total Library Budget

Library Budget	Yes	No
Less than $500,000	8.00%	92.00%
$500,000 to $4 Million	26.92%	73.08%
More than $4 Million	29.41%	70.59%

Table 42.4: Does the library currently own or lease a Samsung Galaxy Broken out by Total Library Budget

Library Budget	Yes	No
Less than $500,000	0.00%	100.00%
$500,000 to $4 Million	0.00%	100.00%
More than $4 Million	5.88%	94.12%

Table 42.5: Does the library currently own or lease a Barnes & Noble Nook Broken out by Total Library Budget

Library Budget	Yes	No
Less than $500,000	16.00%	84.00%
$500,000 to $4 Million	7.69%	92.31%
More than $4 Million	17.65%	82.35%

Table 43: Does the library plan to acquire any of the following within the next year?

Table 43.1: Does the library plan to acquire an Amazon Kindle E-book Reader?

	Yes	No
Entire Sample	8.82%	91.18%

Table 43.2: Does the library plan to acquire a Motorola Xoom?

	Yes	No
Entire Sample	0.00%	100.00%

Table 43.3: Does the library plan to acquire a Samsung Galaxy?

	Yes	No
Entire Sample	0.00%	100.00%

Table 43.4: Does the library plan to acquire a BlackBerry Playbook?

	Yes	No
Entire Sample	0.00%	100.00%

Table 43.5: Does the library plan to acquire a Sony Reader?

	Yes	No
Entire Sample	1.47%	98.53%

Table 43.6: Does the library plan to acquire an Apple iPad?

	Yes	No
Entire Sample	14.71%	85.29%

Table 43.7: Does the library plan to acquire a Franklin eBookMan?

	Yes	No
Entire Sample	0.00%	100.00%

Table 43.8: Does the library plan to acquire a Barnes & Noble Nook?

	Yes	No
Entire Sample	1.47%	98.53%

Table 44: Does the library plan to acquire any of the following within the next year? Broken out by Country

Table 44.1: Does the library plan to acquire an Amazon Kindle E-book Reader? Broken out by Country

Country	Yes	No
United States	8.16%	91.84%
Other	10.53%	89.47%

Table 44.2: Does the library plan to acquire a Sony Reader? Broken out by Country

Country	Yes	No
United States	0.00%	100.00%
Other	5.26%	94.74%

Table 44.3: Does the library plan to acquire an Apple iPad? Broken out by Country

Country	Yes	No
United States	14.29%	85.71%
Other	15.79%	84.21%

Table 44.4: Does the library plan to acquire a Barnes & Noble Nook? Broken out by Country

Country	Yes	No
United States	0.00%	100.00%
Other	5.26%	94.74%

Table 45: Does the library plan to acquire any of the following within the next year? Broken out by Type of Library

Table 43.1: Does the library plan to acquire an Amazon Kindle E-book Reader? Broken out by Type of Library

Type of Library	Yes	No
Public Library	10.53%	89.47%
College Library	9.38%	90.63%
Other	5.88%	94.12%

Table 45.2: Does the library plan to acquire a Sony Reader? Broken out by Type of Library

Type of Library	Yes	No
Public Library	0.00%	100.00%
College Library	3.13%	96.88%
Other	0.00%	100.00%

Table 45.3 Library Plans to Acquire an Apple iPad? Broken out by Type of Library

Type of Library	Yes	No
Public Library	5.26%	94.74%
College Library	28.13%	71.88%
Other	0.00%	100.00%

Table 45.4 Library Plans to Acquire a Barnes & Noble Nook? Broken out by Type of Library

Type of Library	Yes	No
Public Library	0.00%	100.00%
College Library	3.13%	96.88%
Other	0.00%	100.00%

Table 46: Does the library plan to acquire any of the following within the next year? Broken out by Total Library Budget

Table 46.1: Does the library plan to acquire an Amazon Kindle E-book Reader? Broken out by Type of Library

Library Budget	Yes	No
Less than $500,000	12.00%	88.00%
$500,000 to $4 Million	7.69%	92.31%
More than $4 Million	5.88%	94.12%

Table 46.2: Does the library plan to acquire a Sony Reader? Broken out by Type of Library

Library Budget	Yes	No
Less than $500,000	4.00%	96.00%
$500,000 to $4 Million	0.00%	100.00%
More than $4 Million	0.00%	100.00%

Table 46.3: Does the library plan to acquire an Apple iPad? Broken out by Type of Library

Library Budget	Yes	No
Less than $500,000	12.00%	88.00%
$500,000 to $4 Million	19.23%	80.77%
More than $4 Million	11.76%	88.24%

Table 46.4: Does the library plan to acquire a Barnes & Noble Nook? Broken out by Type of Library

Library Budget	Yes	No
Less than $500,000	4.00%	96.00%
$500,000 to $4 Million	0.00%	100.00%
More than $4 Million	0.00%	100.00%

Table 47: How much did or will your library spend on dedicated e-book readers and tablet computers in the specified years?

Table 47.1: How much did the library spend on e-book readers in 2012? (in $US)

	Mean	Median	Minimum	Maximum
Entire Sample	$1,003.21	$0.00	$0.00	$10,000.00

Table 47.2: How much will the library spend on e-book readers in 2013? (in $US)

	Mean	Median	Minimum	Maximum
Entire Sample	$992.86	$0.00	$0.00	$20,000.00

Table 48: How much did or will your library spend on dedicated e-book readers and tablet computers in the specified years? Broken out by Country

Table 48.1: How much did the library spend on e-book readers in 2012? Broken out by Country (in $US)

Country	Mean	Median	Minimum	Maximum
United States	$978.42	$0.00	$0.00	$10,000.00
Other	$1,055.56	$0.00	$0.00	$10,000.00

Table 48.2: How much will the library spend on e-book readers in 2013? Broken out by Country (in $US)

Country	Mean	Median	Minimum	Maximum
United States	$686.84	$0.00	$0.00	$10,000.00
Other	$1,638.89	$0.00	$0.00	$20,000.00

Table 49: How much did or will your library spend on dedicated e-book readers and tablet computers in the specified years? Broken out by Type of Library

Table 49.1: How much did the library spend on e-book readers in 2012? Broken out by Type of Library (in $US)

Type of Library	Mean	Median	Minimum	Maximum
Public Library	$1,500.00	$0.00	$0.00	$10,000.00
College Library	$1,202.96	$0.00	$0.00	$10,000.00
Other	$262.50	$0.00	$0.00	$1,700.00

Table 49.2: How much will the library spend on e-book readers in 2013? Broken out by Type of Library (in $US)

Type of Library	Mean	Median	Minimum	Maximum
Public Library	$546.15	$0.00	$0.00	$3,000.00
College Library	$1,777.78	$0.00	$0.00	$20,000.00
Other	$31.25	$0.00	$0.00	$500.00

Table 50: How much did or will your library spend on dedicated e-book readers and tablet computers in the specified years? Broken out by Total Library Budget

Table 50.1: How much did the library spend on e-book readers in 2012? Broken out by Type of Library Budget (in $US)

Library Budget	Mean	Median	Minimum	Maximum
Less than $500,000	$850.00	$0.00	$0.00	$10,000.00
$500,000 to $4 Million	$758.18	$0.00	$0.00	$5,000.00
More than $4 Million	$1,607.14	$0.00	$0.00	$10,000.00

Table 50.2: How much will the library spend on e-book readers in 2013? Broken out by Type of Library Budget (in $US)

Library Budget	Mean	Median	Minimum	Maximum
Less than $500,000	$1,390.00	$0.00	$0.00	$20,000.00
$500,000 to $4 Million	$681.82	$0.00	$0.00	$10,000.00
More than $4 Million	$914.29	$150.00	$0.00	$3,000.00

CHAPTER 7: PRINT vs ONLINE

Table 51.1: For what percentage of the e-books in the library's collection does the library also have a corresponding print copy?

	Mean	Median	Minimum	Maximum
Entire Sample	28.11%	10.00%	0.00%	100.00%

Table 51.2: For what percentage of the e-books in the library's collection does the library also have a corresponding print copy? Broken out by Country

Country	Mean	Median	Minimum	Maximum
United States	31.14%	10.00%	0.00%	100.00%
Other	21.53%	10.00%	0.00%	85.00%

Table 51.3: For what percentage of the e-books in the library's collection does the library also have a corresponding print copy? Broken out by Type of Library

Type of Library	Mean	Median	Minimum	Maximum
Public Library	50.00%	55.00%	0.00%	100.00%
College Library	19.41%	10.00%	0.00%	100.00%
Other	26.27%	20.00%	0.00%	90.00%

Table 51.4: For what percentage of the e-books in the library's collection does the library also have a corresponding print copy? Broken out by Total Library Budget

Library Budget	Mean	Median	Minimum	Maximum
Less than $500,000	18.42%	5.00%	0.00%	90.00%
$500,000 to $4 Million	26.76%	10.00%	0.00%	95.00%
More than $4 Million	43.29%	25.00%	2.00%	100.00%

Table 52.1: If the library has an endowment, bequest, or specially dedicated fund of any kind for books, may this fund be used for the purchase of e-books?

	We have an endowment for books but cannot use it for e-books	We have an endowment for books and we can use it for e-books	We have an endowment especially for e-books and other electronic resources	We have no such endowment for books of any kind
Entire Sample	14.52%	19.35%	1.61%	64.52%

Table 52.2: If the library has an endowment, bequest, or specially dedicated fund of any kind for books, may this fund be used for the purchase of e-books? Broken out by Country

Country	We have an endowment for books but cannot use it for e-books	We have an endowment for books and we can use it for e-books	We have an endowment especially for e-books and other electronic resources	We have no such endowment for books of any kind
United States	16.28%	23.26%	2.33%	58.14%
Other	10.53%	10.53%	0.00%	78.95%

Table 52.3: If the library has an endowment, bequest, or specially dedicated fund of any kind for books, may this fund be used for the purchase of e-books? Broken out by Type of Library

Type of Library	We have an endowment for books but cannot use it for e-books	We have an endowment for books and we can use it for e-books	We have an endowment especially for e-books and other electronic resources	We have no such endowment for books of any kind
Public Library	13.33%	20.00%	6.67%	60.00%
College Library	16.67%	26.67%	0.00%	56.67%
Other	11.76%	5.88%	0.00%	82.35%

Table 52.4: If the library has an endowment, bequest, or specially dedicated fund of any kind for books, may this fund be used for the purchase of e-books? Broken out by Total Library Budget

Library Budget	We have an endowment for books but cannot use it for e-books	We have an endowment for books and we can use it for e-books	We have an endowment especially for e-books and other electronic resources	We have no such endowment for books of any kind
Less than $500,000	9.52%	14.29%	0.00%	76.19%
$500,000 to $4 Million	16.00%	16.00%	4.00%	64.00%
More than $4 Million	18.75%	31.25%	0.00%	50.00%

CHAPTER 8: E-BOOKS AND ELECTRONIC COURSE RESERVE

Table 53.1: How would you describe your use of e-books for course reserve?

	Not Used	Scant Use	Modest Use	Significant Use
Entire Sample	60.98%	9.76%	21.95%	7.32%

Table 53.2: How would you describe your use of e-books for course reserve? Broken out by Country

Country	Not Used	Scant Use	Modest Use	Significant Use
United States	75.86%	10.34%	13.79%	0.00%
Other	25.00%	8.33%	41.67%	25.00%

Table 53.3: How would you describe your use of e-books for course reserve? Broken out by Type of Library

Type of Library	Not Used	Scant Use	Modest Use	Significant Use
Public Library	83.33%	0.00%	16.67%	0.00%
College Library	60.00%	10.00%	20.00%	10.00%
Other	40.00%	20.00%	40.00%	0.00%

Table 53.4: How would you describe your use of e-books for course reserve? Broken out by Total Library Budget

Library Budget	Not Used	Scant Use	Modest Use	Significant Use
Less than $500,000	57.14%	7.14%	35.71%	0.00%
$500,000 to $4 Million	82.35%	11.76%	5.88%	0.00%
More than $4 Million	30.00%	10.00%	30.00%	30.00%

Over the past two years, has the use of e-books for electronic course reserves increased or decreased? What are the current constraints on use and what do you expect for the near future?

1. We haven't used e-books for electronic course reserve. Our course reserve system is managed within the course management system interface (Blackboard). A current constraint is faculty knowing about the e-books we have that they could direct students to within Blackboard for electronic course reserve.
2. This is an area we would like to expand but we need to ensure there are appropriate titles and licenses available for a course reserve option
3. Increased when we can purchase the title for unlimited use to support from 30-100 students
4. Increased. Faculty is not going outside of texts much.
5. Yes, the use of e-books have considerably increased
6. It is increasing but very slowly because there is not enough relevant literature
7. I only see constraints on textbook type e-books that are placed on reserves
8. Teaching staff have a fixed set of texts for use. The majority of these texts are not offered in e-format for library purchase.
9. Increased. Constraint is lack of access in regards to ability to purchase and cost.
10. We are currently in the beginning stages of exploring the possibility of introducing e-books for course reserves. We will need to have conversations with our faculty and our students as to use, expectations, and use in the classroom and for exams. Currently, we use exam software that prevents extra materials from being used on a student's laptop while taking an exam. Some exams are open book but closed other materials. When the exam software is used an e-book would need to be used with another device with the possibility for other materials to be used. That conflict needs to be resolved.
11. Not an academic library, no course reserve
12. Currently patrons need to borrow the device to read e-books – they would prefer to download onto their own device, but currently we do not offer this service
13. Increasing. Computer access can still be a constraint on use but it is improving.
14. Not used
15. It has increased. The constraint is that many of the books which our students need most are not available as e-books.
16. Increased from 0 to 90 or so per month
17. E-books are not used for course reserves due to DRACONIC DRM issues
18. Increased. Main constraint is funding.
19. Increased. Constraints include single-use titles, and uncertainty that subscription titles will be available long-term.
20. Students complain about not having platforms they prefer to download e-books to. They also complain about problems downloading e-books and difficulty of having to deal with publishers.
21. Not in the cards for us at present
22. Increased and there are no constraints on use
23. We haven't used it. Biggest constraint is typically the items on reserve are not available as e-books. Over time, as more e-books become available, I expect we will use them on reserve.
24. Limited users, contractual constraints, copyright limitations
25. Instructors may select journal articles for e-reserve, but they don't select e-books for reserve. E-books are more likely to be on a reading list and students are expected to find them on their own in our collection.
26. Use has remained the same
27. We have not developed a good workflow to incorporate e-books in course reserves

CHAPTER 9: E-DIRECTORIES

Table 54.1: How much did the library spend on electronic and internet versions of directories in the past year? (in $US)

	Mean	Median	Minimum	Maximum
Entire Sample	$2,820.47	$0.00	$0.00	$70,000.00

Table 54.2: How much did the library spend on electronic and internet versions of directories in the past year? Broken out by Country (in $US)

Country	Mean	Median	Minimum	Maximum
United States	$3,267.19	$0.00	$0.00	$70,000.00
Other	$1,867.47	$0.00	$0.00	$12,000.00

Table 54.3: How much did the library spend on electronic and internet versions of directories in the past year? Broken out by Type of Library (in $US)

Type of Library	Mean	Median	Minimum	Maximum
Public Library	$8,750.00	$0.00	$0.00	$70,000.00
College Library	$1,820.45	$0.00	$0.00	$25,000.00
Other	$1,324.24	$0.00	$0.00	$12,000.00

Table 54.4: How much did the library spend on electronic and internet versions of directories in the past year? Broken out by Total Library Budget (in $US)

Library Budget	Mean	Median	Minimum	Maximum
Less than $500,000	$134.21	$0.00	$0.00	$2,000.00
$500,000 to $4 Million	$4,626.32	$0.00	$0.00	$70,000.00
More than $4 Million	$4,679.11	$2,000.00	$0.00	$25,000.00

Table 55.1: How much does the library plan to spend on electronic and internet versions of directories in the upcoming year? (in $US)

	Mean	Median	Minimum	Maximum
Entire Sample	$2,824.21	$0.00	$0.00	$70,000.00

Table 55.2: How much does the library plan to spend on electronic and internet versions of directories in the upcoming year? Broken out by Country (in $US)

Country	Mean	Median	Minimum	Maximum
United States	$3,168.18	$0.00	$0.00	$70,000.00
Other	$2,067.47	$0.00	$0.00	$15,000.00

Table 55.3: How much does the library plan to spend on electronic and internet versions of directories in the upcoming year? Broken out by Type of Library (in $US)

Type of Library	Mean	Median	Minimum	Maximum
Public Library	$8,750.00	$0.00	$0.00	$70,000.00
College Library	$1,697.83	$0.00	$0.00	$26,000.00
Other	$1,559.53	$0.00	$0.00	$15,000.00

Table 55.4: How much does the library plan to spend on electronic and internet versions of directories in the upcoming year? Broken out by Total Library Budget (in $US)

Library Budget	Mean	Median	Minimum	Maximum
Less than $500,000	$186.84	$0.00	$0.00	$2,000.00
$500,000 to $4 Million	$4,445.00	$0.00	$0.00	$70,000.00
More than $4 Million	$4,790.22	$2,000.00	$0.00	$26,000.00

CHAPTER 10: PRICING

Table 56: In the past year what has been the library's experience with changes in the prices of e-books relative to the changes in price of traditional print books, online databases of full text articles, and other resources specified below?

Table 56.1: How has the price of e-books changed relative to the change in price of print books?

	Price increases have been about the same	Price increases have been higher for e-books	Our e-book prices have not increased
Entire Sample	33.33%	44.44%	22.22%

Table 56.2: How has the price of e-books changed relative to the change in price of online full text databases?

	Price increases have been about the same	Price increases have been higher for e-books	Our e-book prices have not increased
Entire Sample	44.44%	26.67%	28.89%

Table 57: In the past year what has been the library's experience with changes in the prices of e-books relative to the changes in price of traditional print books, online databases of full text articles, and other resources specified below? Broken out by Country

Table 57.1: How has the price of e-books changed relative to the change in price of print books? Broken out by Country

Country	Price increases have been about the same	Price increases have been higher for e-books	Our e-book prices have not increased
United States	25.81%	54.84%	19.35%
Other	50.00%	21.43%	28.57%

Table 57.2: How has the price of e-books changed relative to the change in price of online full text databases? Broken out by Country

Country	Price increases have been about the same	Price increases have been higher for e-books	Our e-book prices have not increased
United States	35.48%	32.26%	32.26%
Other	64.29%	14.29%	21.43%

Table 58: In the past year what has been the library's experience with changes in the prices of e-books relative to the changes in price of traditional print books, online databases of full text articles, and other resources specified below? Broken out by Type of Library

Table 58.1: How has the price of e-books changed relative to the change in price of print books? Broken out by Type of Library

Type of Library	Price increases have been about the same	Price increases have been higher for e-books	Our e-book prices have not increased
Public Library	11.11%	77.78%	11.11%
College Library	39.13%	43.48%	17.39%
Other	38.46%	23.08%	38.46%

Table 58.2: How has the price of e-books changed relative to the change in price of online full text databases? Broken out by Type of Library

Type of Library	Price increases have been about the same	Price increases have been higher for e-books	Our e-book prices have not increased
Public Library	22.22%	55.56%	22.22%
College Library	47.83%	21.74%	30.43%
Other	53.85%	15.38%	30.77%

Table 59: In the past year what has been the library's experience with changes in the prices of e-books relative to the changes in price of traditional print books, online databases of full text articles, and other resources specified below? Broken out by Total Library Budget

Table 59.1: How has the price of e-books changed relative to the change in price of print books? Broken out by Total Library Budget

Library Budget	Price increases have been about the same	Price increases have been higher for e-books	Our e-book prices have not increased
Less than $500,000	43.75%	31.25%	25.00%
$500,000 to $4 Million	18.75%	50.00%	31.25%
More than $4 Million	38.46%	53.85%	7.69%

Table 59.2: How has the price of e-books changed relative to the change in price of online full text databases?

Library Budget	Price increases have been about the same	Price increases have been higher for e-books	Our e-book prices have not increased
Less than $500,000	50.00%	18.75%	31.25%
$500,000 to $4 Million	31.25%	37.50%	31.25%

Table 60.1: What was the average percentage change in e-book prices that your organization paid in the last year?

	Mean	Median	Minimum	Maximum
Entire Sample	17.93%	5.00%	0.00%	200.00%

Table 60.2: What was the average percentage change in e-book prices that your organization paid in the last year? Broken out by Country

Country	Mean	Median	Minimum	Maximum
United States	25.23%	5.50%	0.00%	200.00%
Other	4.80%	4.50%	0.00%	15.00%

Table 60.3: What was the average percentage change in e-book prices that your organization paid in the last year? Broken out by Type of Library

Type of Library	Mean	Median	Minimum	Maximum
Public Library	54.17%	12.50%	0.00%	200.00%
College Library	10.39%	5.00%	0.00%	40.00%
Other	4.67%	4.00%	0.00%	15.00%

Table 60.4: What was the average percentage change in e-book prices that your organization paid in the last year? Broken out by Total Library Budget

Library Budget	Mean	Median	Minimum	Maximum
Less than $500,000	4.01%	5.00%	0.00%	15.00%
$500,000 to $4 Million	21.80%	11.00%	0.00%	100.00%
More than $4 Million	34.29%	5.00%	4.00%	200.00%

CHAPTER 11: E-BOOK COLLECTION PLANNING

Discuss your library's e-book collection strategy. How fast do you expect your e-book collection to grow? Has it led to reduced spending on traditional books? Do your library patrons make use of e-book searching capacity? How will e-books affect your cataloging and information literacy strategies?

1. We are starting with electronic reference books. We expect our electronic reference holdings to grow each year. We are extensively weeding print reference and replacing/updating many of the titles with electronic reference. We have not reduced spending on print books yet. Yes, students make use of e-book searching abilities. We have had to rework the process of cataloging, processing invoices and troubleshooting, and are still refining the work-flow process.

2. Currently our collection strategy is patron initiated mostly, but we would prefer to move to an "e-book first" model where we buy e-books over print books if possible. We expect the e-book collection to grow by about 50% (from a rather small collection now), but would prefer to wait until a viable solution is found to the issues of e-book ownership, e-reader compatibility, and ADA access. Patrons are highly interested in e-books, but find the searching and downloading difficult and full of hassles. E-books require a slightly different cataloging strategy, but should not affect things greatly. For information literacy, e-books often make it easier to relate the worth of more scholarly resources since it can be searched easily and quickly online like a page of the Internet.

3. E-book collection growth will depend on the budget, but will not necessarily result in reduced print purchases. We note an interest in the ability to download e-books to devices, i.e. iPads, etc., and have queried EBSCO and ProQuest about apps. Some patrons use e-book searching in support of their research efforts. International students are eager for e-book access to English language titles.

4. Just learning to add e-books to the catalog. Will add 3M to Polaris catalog in 2013. Until the six publishers play well with libraries, it is a waste of taxpayers' money to spend it on resources they don't want. Less print yes.

5. We have increased demand for e-books and e-audiobooks, but still have the same demand for print and audiobooks in traditional formats as well. We have seen a slight decrease in spending on reference books in print as we get more of these resources in electronic format, but have not decreased our other print budgets.

6. We expect demand for e-books to massively increase, but our book budget is not expected to increase, in fact it is significantly lower this fiscal year than last. We have redirected a small amount of funding from print books to e-books, but ultimately we will probably lose e-book patrons because we must maintain our print collection which serves the larger number of patrons. We are still considering options regarding inclusion of e-books in the main library catalog.

7. This is the beginning of the collection, but yes, purchase of e-books will reduce spending on traditional books.

8. Our loosely organized consortium is trying to purchase popular fiction titles and buying multiple copies in order to get the holds down

9. We are reducing spending on databases, not print

10. Our collection will increase each year in e-books and users are asking themselves digital versions and not printed

11. E-book growth by 10% per year, reduction in print book spending by 10%. Greater amount of external data in cataloging.

12. No strategy or purchases at this time, but looking into EBSCO e-books

13. People responsible for promoting and marketing the e-books have not, and will continue not to market them. Usage is very low. Talking about ordering more, but really a waste of money without any sort of promotion. Hasn't been a library budget to purchase books for more than 10 years. Chargebacks are done to staff budgets. Don't use it much, as it isn't promoted. Cataloging and information literacy strategy shouldn't be affected.

14. Spending on e-books has grown and led to reduced spending on traditional books. We try to have as many records as possible for e-books in our catalogue.

15. We are targeting PDA or DDA use of e-books. It currently has not nor will it totally replace print books until a respectable lending and borrowing license can be arranged and worked out. Right now e-books can only be used by our campus users, which is frustrating and unsustainable in the bigger spirit of libraries due to their public good purpose! Cataloging will refocus to repairing what we see as poor quality MARC records that are supplied by the vendors and publishers. E-books will still need the normal information literacy instruction strategies and more as you can embed in course management systems that much more easily or in the case of PDA, have that much more available for users!

16. E-books will grow while print publications will be reduced. E-titles are already provided in the library catalog and searchable from our discovery service.

17. Quick growth with reduced traditional collection. Patrons have increased usage, but "friction" is hard to overcome with complicated procedures for different devices.

18. We are still at the beginning stages of considering e-books and will be looking at cost very closely as well as how it will affect our teaching and staff workflow

19. We are very specific with our e-book purchasing. We will buy if the price is suitable, it fits our subject matter needs, and the licensing conditions permit our usage models. Also depends on DRM, as DRM software is not enabled within our organization, and we can't currently get it installed by our IT department.

20. No formal strategy. E-books are purchased when an item is needed quickly or when there is a significant cost decrease.

21. We buy e-versions of textbooks when available via a corporate account and plan on building our e-book collection. All e-books are entered into our ILS.

22. Slow growth. Spending on print books continues because it is a dedicated budget. E-books are just a part of the bigger picture, not a specific thing that we greatly seek or avoid. More would be good but we need appropriate funding to grow.

23. We will buy more e-books and fewer traditional books. We are creating subject pages to help our users find the e-books. Our users love our e-books. We download MARC records which saves us cataloging time.

24. Limited to funds provided by our Foundation. This is our first year (began November 2012) so we have yet to see what will happen.

25. E-books are growing at a faster rate than books because publishers can create affordable collections at a deep discount. Our patrons do make use of e-books and searching for, and use of is part of the IL sessions.

26. Growth projected to be 10%. No reduced spending on traditional books. Patrons make use of e-book searching.

27. We had an extensive collection of Medical and Nursing e-books from OVID for three years which was hardly used despite intensive and repeated marketing. Our patrons are predominately into print books, the e-books we have these days are either part of our database package, through the State Library consortium, or are online access with print book purchase. I would love to remove the print collection and replace it with multiple tablets available for checkout and have a plethora of online books, but I don't have the clientele or administration willing to embrace this change yet.

28. Considering PDA purchase models as this will be primarily a virtual library

29. Our e-book collection has grown steadily since 2004 and I expect it to grow faster in future as we try to spend more on e-books. Traditional book spending has not decreased significantly yet, although I expect it to decline over the next few years – more so in science and technology areas but to some extent in all subjects. Our patrons make great use of e-book searching and teaching students how to make best use of e-books is a major focus of our information literacy strategy already. Our bought-in e-books are all fully catalogued and available just like our print books.

30. Our e-books are done through the region so we don't have control over them but our users are increasing

31. We expect the collection to grow when publishers finally relent and make e-books ready for purchase at the same time as print version is available. No reduced spending on print because publishers do not issue e-books until 6-10 months after release of the print. As a medical library we need to have the most current information. This publishing strategy is counterproductive to the needs of medical libraries. Patrons like the e-books searching that we have in place. E-books will not affect cataloging and information literacy strategies.

32. E-book collections for specialist courses (HND) as alternative to hard copy. Some level-3 textbooks, where hardcopy is also available.

33. Steady growth in e-book purchases, but there is an inherent tension with print format. This varies according to subject area.

34. We will begin offering Demand Driven Acquisitions in 2013 – we expect to see an increase in our e-book purchasing, which will ultimately lead to a decrease in print book purchasing. For cataloging, e-books require more file uploading and modifying on a large scale rather than cataloging individual titles. We have added sections about using e-books for our IL sessions. This has been happening on the fly – to date, we do not have a strategy.

35. Our only stated strategy at this time is to try and use as many e-books for texts as possible

36. When given a choice, we normally purchase the e-book instead of print. We still have a print approval plan. Collection will increase as more titles become available in the e-format. Also, we must have funds for the purchase of e-books. No use of e-book searching capacity. No real effect on cataloging.

37. We are transitioning to 90 e-books over 3 years. It is not uncommon to have 30 e-books with more usage in 1 month than the entire library of 1200 print books had in 1 year. We will continue to purchase fewer print books and only what we cannot find in e-book format. The searching functionality on R2R platform is well used. Information literacy – awareness and access at "point of need". The platform is intuitive for initial use. Once user is hooked, reel them in to teach advanced options.

38. Right now we don't have one. We have the ability to borrow via our membership in the New York Law Institute.

39. I expect e-book collection will slowly increase, with reduced spending on traditional books. The patrons do not make full use of the e-book searching capacity. I don't anticipate problems with cataloging/information literacy.

40. We have no strategy at the moment since it is new for us

41. MARC records for e-books are loaded into our online catalog. Expect moderate growth as aggregators add titles. E-books have had a small impact (decrease) in spending on print books. Most patrons like the searching features that come with having a book online.

42. We do not purchase e-books directly. All offerings are through the State library and Archives READS site. This has not affected our book circulation.

43. Expect it to grow because the administration wants the library's space and they are anxious for us to get as many e-books as possible.

44. The library intends to expand our e-book collecting in 2013. Over the past six years e-book collecting has been tentative, but we are now moving towards a more systematic approach. This will occur by starting an e-preferred purchasing arrangement for US and UK publications through YBP Library Services (our current print supplier). We expect to reduce spending on print publications; we will not be duplicating the purchase of print and online monographs. Our library patrons are very gradually embracing e-books, most are dissatisfied with DRM. Catalogue records for e-books will be purchased through YBP. We expect to continue to incorporate e-books in our lifelong learning programs, referring to them in subject guides, blocks etc.

45. We plan on getting e-books over books. We have spent a little less for traditional books and used the moneys for e-book collections, i.e. Ebrary, EBSCO. Patrons do use e-book searching. Batch loading of MARC records makes cataloging easier. The whole of information literacy has changed with the changes in technology, i.e. card catalogs to online catalogs, online catalogs to cloud computing.

46. It will grow very fast because we now have a lot of subscriptions to e-book collections. More than purchase titles.

47. Spending on e-books has cut into spending on print books. It takes more time to explain to patrons how to use the different e-book formats.

48. Hope to build e-book use this year. Will look for good additions, but do not expect to find products that fit our need. Will be teaching more about online search strategies.

49. Slowly, we are in the first phase

50. Our catalogers have failed to load MARC records for e-books in a timely manner, so we have given up on buying e-books

51. It is expected to grow quickly. Yes, they are in the regular catalog so searching is the same.

Do internet enabled tablets such as the Apple iPad, the HP Slate, or any of the Google Tablets figure in your e-book planning? Will you use the e-book capabilities of these devices in your library in the near future?

1. Not in the near future, but eventually we will purchase some
2. They do figure in, but with limited resources we will not be tailoring any of our efforts to these specific devices
3. iPad devices may be utilized by future classes. Testing with IT department, along with possible use of iTunes University features.
4. The only way we use tablets/gadgets are in the classroom to help people with downloading. Our patrons are wealthy and can afford their own equipment. We are lucky!
5. We expect to acquire at least 1-2 iPads and a Kindle Fire in order to offer ADA-accessible alternatives to the 12 B&N Nooks we will be circulating this year
6. Possibly for reference services
7. Not at this time
8. Yes, we anticipate they will outsell e-book readers
9. Yes, we currently lend e-readers and will continue to introduce more devices to the collection. This facilitates the use of e-books for students and teachers.
10. No
11. No
12. No
13. Not relevant
14. Yes, as long as the option is provided for library to offer e-titles on the tablets
15. Tablets are easier to use with apps

16. Depending on our decisions as to e-books and what our internal survey results show as to student's access to these devices and their interest in e-books for course books, etc.
17. No. Organization's IT and security policies do not permit the use of these devices in our environment, so no point considering until the organizational policies change.
18. Undecided
19. I would load in e-books into our iPads if a corporate account was available to do so
20. Users are starting to show up using these devices but still not many. They will definitely increase over time.
21. We use those devices to instruct users. We will not be lending out the devices.
22. Hope to apply for grants/funding to supply lendable tablets/devices for patrons to try before purchasing their own as popularity of e-books grows
23. No
24. Yes
25. Tablet considerations very important. Agnostic e-books will be essential.
26. We are unlikely to provide tablets ourselves, but I expect individual students to appear with more of these in future. We would want our aggregator e-books to be compatible.
27. Perhaps the iPad will, but not until publishers change their business model of selling out the print runs before issuing e-book versions
28. Yes, we will be expanding this area
29. No
30. Currently, no. We always have our eye on the future – I'm just not certain that the people at the top are making good use of the knowledge of those who are on the ground.
31. There is serious discussion of using some type of tablet (for all students)
32. No
33. We experimented with Kindles (Q13) and found that "users" fit into one of two categories: (1) liked Kindle so much that they wouldn't return it or, (2) never got around to using it though they intended to so they wouldn't return it. Kindle books have limited access (up to 4 or 5 according to some publishers: 1 user for others). Thus, we won't spend money on this technology.
34. Attorneys will have the option of purchasing e-book versions for their personal use
35. No
36. Yes
37. E-book strategy is independent of device
38. No
39. No, these items do not
40. The library encourages users to bring in their own devices and to use our free on-site wireless services for all electronic resources including e-books. We do not intend to offer internet enabled devices to library users.
41. Probably not. Because many patrons use iPads and iPhones, etc., they will be able to take advantage of the ability to access library e-books. It's not worth the expense or the hassle of getting similar devices for the library.
42. Yes
43. Looking for e-books for libraries that work across tablets with ease
44. Tablets will be a factor only as our patrons are using them to access online resources. We do not plan anything special because of them. We do plan to do more alternative configurations for small mobile devices, such as iPhones.
45. No

Table 61.1: Has your library purchased e-books from well-known websites, newspapers and other media outlets such as The New York Times and the Huffington Post, which have started to publish their own e-books?

	Yes	No
Entire Sample	1.72%	98.28%

Table 61.2: Has your library purchased e-books from well-known websites, newspapers and other media outlets such as The New York Times and the Huffington Post, which have started to publish their own e-books? Broken out by Country

Country	Yes	No
United States	0.00%	100.00%
Other	5.88%	94.12%

Table 61.3: Has your library purchased e-books from well-known websites, newspapers and other media outlets such as The New York Times and the Huffington Post, which have started to publish their own e-books? Broken out by Type of Library

Type of Library	Yes	No
Public Library	0.00%	100.00%
College Library	3.45%	96.55%
Other	0.00%	100.00%

Table 61.4: Has your library purchased e-books from well-known websites, newspapers and other media outlets such as The New York Times and the Huffington Post, which have started to publish their own e-books? Broken out by Total Library Budget

Library Budget	Yes	No
Less than $500,000	5.00%	95.00%
$500,000 to $4 Million	0.00%	100.00%
More than $4 Million	0.00%	100.00%

CHAPTER 12: E-TEXTBOOKS

Describe your library's attempts to license e-textbooks. Have you approached or negotiated with any textbook publishers over e-book rights? What kind of results have you achieved? Do you have plans or a strategy in this area?

1. Our library does not collect textbooks, print or electronic
2. We have an e-textbook committee that has analyzed the different options, met with various vendors, and tried several "sandbox" e-textbooks. However, since an e-textbook option from a publisher locks you into a contract that puts limits on our options, we are not likely to enter into an agreement in the near term.
3. Little to no use of textbooks
4. We are waiting to see what else comes along before we deal with e-book rights
5. None
6. We have not negotiated with any publisher and have no plans for now
7. We will consider it in 2013
8. No, but more and more disciplines are starting to initiate discussions about this. This is a bigger campus issue as the administration and bookstore need to see the overall impact and cost. So, we are just in the initial phase of such a thing. Again, until publishers mature in their thinking about how they price and handle borrowing and loaning of e-books, there is little of interest to academic libraries.
9. There was no agreeable outcome on providing e-textbooks
10. The school is considering exploring this approach. The conversation is just beginning.
11. Not as of yet, but will plan to do so in the future
12. We have just accepted what was readily available, mainly in packages. We cancelled one package that was too expensive, have a few within other general packages and are left with just one direct sub.
13. No luck negotiating. We hope that EBSCO and the aggregators will get a larger collection of e-books.
14. Not really applicable to us as a public library – it is not our mission to supply textbooks
15. We have not approached specific publishers, but have told aggregators and publishing reps who visit that it is a problem that many textbooks on our reading lists are not available as e-books via our aggregators, e.g. W. W. Norton and Pearson Longman
16. Publishers will not license e-textbooks to libraries. The several times that I have licensed them, I've been hit with DRACONIC DRM issues and huge price increases over what the publisher sells to students. Until publishers become library friendly, we will not be pursuing plans for e-textbooks. It's not worth my time or effort.
17. We have not attempted this to date. Nor are there plans to do so in the immediate future.
18. Currently, none. We discuss this from time to time, but our budget is not likely to allow it in the near future.
19. We do not purchase textbooks
20. Tried to purchase one, but was told they came in a bundle and the price was too high. No plans to pursue this.
21. Only investigated with some publishers. It is a possibility that we will purchase e-textbooks in the future.
22. We are currently looking into this as the college is moving to expand e-textbooks
23. The library has not attempted to license e-textbooks. These publications are outside of our collection development policy.
24. We don't mess with textbooks

25. Not at this time
26. None
27. None
28. E-textbooks are not part of our collection priorities. We do not purchase required texts.
29. Not at this time
30. We have not done this
31. No, we would be interested in general although we do not purchase textbooks as per collection policy

Table 62: How much did your library spend on purchasing, leasing or licensing e-textbooks in the years listed below?

Table 62.1: How much did your library spend on purchasing, leasing or licensing e-textbooks in 2012? (in $US)

	Mean	Median	Minimum	Maximum
Entire Sample	$1,041.53	$0.00	$0.00	$40,000.00

Table 62.2: How much will your library spend on purchasing, leasing or licensing e-textbooks in 2013? (in $US)

	Mean	Median	Minimum	Maximum
Entire Sample	$1,528.09	$0.00	$0.00	$40,000.00

Table 63: How much did your library spend on purchasing, leasing or licensing e-textbooks in the years listed below? Broken out by Country

Table 63.1: How much did your library spend on purchasing, leasing or licensing e-textbooks in 2012? Broken out by Country (in $US)

Country	Mean	Median	Minimum	Maximum
United States	$30.30	$0.00	$0.00	$1,000.00
Other	$3,425.14	$0.00	$0.00	$40,000.00

Table 63.2: How much will your library spend on purchasing, leasing or licensing e-textbooks in 2013? Broken out by Country (in $US)

Country	Mean	Median	Minimum	Maximum
United States	$333.33	$0.00	$0.00	$10,000.00
Other	$4,344.29	$0.00	$0.00	$40,000.00

Table 64: How much did your library spend on purchasing, leasing or licensing e-textbooks in the years listed below? Broken out by Type of Library

Table 64.1: How much did your library spend on purchasing, leasing or licensing e-textbooks in 2012? Broken out by Type of Library (in $US)

Type of Library	Mean	Median	Minimum	Maximum
Public Library	$0.00	$0.00	$0.00	$0.00
College Library	$250.00	$0.00	$0.00	$5,000.00
Other	$3,068.00	$0.00	$0.00	$40,000.00

Table 64.2: How much will your library spend on purchasing, leasing or licensing e-textbooks in 2013? Broken out by Type of Library (in $US)

Type of Library	Mean	Median	Minimum	Maximum
Public Library	$1,111.11	$0.00	$0.00	$10,000.00
College Library	$875.00	$0.00	$0.00	$20,000.00
Other	$2,915.71	$0.00	$0.00	$40,000.00

Table 65: How much did your library spend on purchasing, leasing or licensing e-textbooks in the years listed below? Broken out by Total Library Budget

Table 65.1: How much did your library spend on purchasing, leasing or licensing e-textbooks in 2012? Broken out by Total Library Budget (in $US)

Library Budget	Mean	Median	Minimum	Maximum
Less than $500,000	$596.80	$0.00	$0.00	$5,000.00
$500,000 to $4 Million	$1,904.76	$0.00	$0.00	$40,000.00
More than $4 Million	$0.00	$0.00	$0.00	$0.00

Table 65.2: How much will your library spend on purchasing, leasing or licensing e-textbooks in 2013? Broken out by Total Library Budget (in $US)

Library Budget	Mean	Median	Minimum	Maximum
Less than $500,000	$1,454.67	$0.00	$0.00	$20,000.00
$500,000 to $4 Million	$2,380.95	$0.00	$0.00	$40,000.00
More than $4 Million	$0.00	$0.00	$0.00	$0.00

Made in the USA
Lexington, KY
15 May 2013